GOVERNMENT PROCEDURES AND OPERATIONS

THE NEW MARKETS TAX CREDIT

BACKGROUND, CONSIDERATIONS AND ISSUES

Government Procedures and Operations

Additional books in this series can be found on Nova's website under the Series tab.

Additional e-books in this series can be found on Nova's website under the e-book tab.

GOVERNMENT PROCEDURES AND OPERATIONS

THE NEW MARKETS TAX CREDIT

BACKGROUND, CONSIDERATIONS AND ISSUES

MARLIN BARRETT
EDITOR

nova publishers
New York

For permission to use material from this book please contact us:
Telephone 631-231-7269; Fax 631-231-8175
Web Site: http://www.novapublishers.com

Library of Congress Cataloging-in-Publication Data

ISBN: 978-1-63463-644-5

Published by Nova Science Publishers, Inc. † New York

CONTENTS

PREFACE

This book describes the New Markets Tax Credit Program and the major considerations banks may need to address when using the tax credits to support community and economic development activities. The book examines the primary opportunities and risks associated with the use of NMTCs and discusses the methods used by national banks and federal savings associations (collectively, banks) to structure transactions and use the credits effectively.

Chapter 1 – The New Markets Tax Credit (NMTC) is a non-refundable tax credit intended to encourage private capital investment in eligible, impoverished, low-income communities. NMTCs are allocated by the Community Development Financial Institutions Fund (CDFI), a bureau within the United States Department of the Treasury, under a competitive application process. Investors who make qualified equity investments reduce their federal income tax liability by claiming the credit. The NMTC program, enacted in 2000, is currently authorized to allocate $33 billion through the end of 2011. To date, the CDFI has exhausted 664 awards totaling $33 billion in NMTC allocation authority. In spite of this, demand for allocations remains strong. For the 2012 NMTC round, requests of nearly $22 billion were made, though any awards are subject to congressional action extending or reauthorizing the program. The most recent program extensions were made in the 111th and 112th Congresses. The American Recovery and Reinvestment Tax Act of 2009, P.L. 111-5, increased the NMTC allocation for 2008 and 2009 to $5 billion from $3.5 billion. Further, the Tax Relief, Unemployment Insurance Reauthorization, and Job Creation Act of 2010 (P.L. 111-312) extended the NMTC authorization through 2011 at $3.5 billion per year. Most recently, the American Taxpayer Relief Act of 2012 (P.L. 112-240) extended the NMTC authorization for 2012 and 2013 at $3.5 billion per year.

Chapter 2 – This *Insights* report describes the New Markets Tax Credit (NMTC) Program and the major considerations banks may need to address when using the tax credits to support community and economic development activities. The report examines the primary opportunities and risks associated with the use of NMTCs and discusses the methods used by national banks and federal savings associations (collectively, banks) to structure transactions and use the credits effectively. The report addresses banks' participation in the NMTC Program as investors, as recipients of the tax credits (allocatees), and as leverage lenders. The information in this report was obtained from a variety of sources, including banks, nonsupervised financial intermediaries, investment fund advisers, and others that actively use NMTCs to finance a diverse range of activities. This information represents our understanding of federal income tax laws and regulations but does not constitute tax advice. Banks should consult their tax advisers about the tax treatments described in this report and the consequences that may apply to their own transactions. Project summaries of several NMTC transactions are included in a case study in appendix A. Appendix B presents a glossary of terms about the NMTC Program. The resource directory in appendix C contains sources of additional information on the program.

Chapter 3 – In recent years, private investors have claimed more than $1 billion in NMTCs annually. The credits are combined with private loans and other public funds to support investments in low- income communities. GAO was asked to review the financial structure of NMTCs. This report assesses: (1) the complexity and transparency of NMTC financial structures and controls over the size of federal subsidies; (2) what is known about the types and amounts of fees and other costs of the financial structures; (3) what is known about the equity remaining in low-income community businesses after the 7-year credit period; and (4) what is known about NMTC project failure rates. GAO reviewed Treasury NMTC data and surveyed CDEs that allocated credits to 305 projects in 2010-2012.

Chapter 4 – The Treasury Department's Community Development Financial Institutions (CDFI) Fund awarded $26 billion in New Markets Tax Credits (NMTC) through 2009 for investment in low-income communities. The NMTC allows investors to claim a tax credit totaling 39 percent of their investment in Community Development Entities (CDE) over 7 years which CDEs reinvest in qualified communities. This mandated report (1) describes where and how CDEs are using NMTCs, (2) assesses how CDEs use NMTCs to offer favorable financing terms to low-income community businesses and describes options for simplifying the NMTC, (3) describes how, if at all,

NMTC investments support low-income community development, and (4) determines how effective IRS and the CDFI Fund have been in monitoring NMTC compliance. GAO analyzed CDFI Fund and CDE data, did case studies of CDEs, and interviewed relevant experts.

In: The New Markets Tax Credit
Editor: Marlin Barrett
ISBN: 978-1-63463-644-5

Chapter 1

NEW MARKETS TAX CREDIT: AN INTRODUCTION*

Donald J. Marples and Sean Lowry

SUMMARY

The New Markets Tax Credit (NMTC) is a non-refundable tax credit intended to encourage private capital investment in eligible, impoverished, low-income communities. NMTCs are allocated by the Community Development Financial Institutions Fund (CDFI), a bureau within the United States Department of the Treasury, under a competitive application process. Investors who make qualified equity investments reduce their federal income tax liability by claiming the credit. The NMTC program, enacted in 2000, is currently authorized to allocate $33 billion through the end of 2011. To date, the CDFI has exhausted 664 awards totaling $33 billion in NMTC allocation authority. In spite of this, demand for allocations remains strong. For the 2012 NMTC round, requests of nearly $22 billion were made, though any awards are subject to congressional action extending or reauthorizing the program.

The most recent program extensions were made in the 111th and 112th Congresses. The American Recovery and Reinvestment Tax Act of 2009, P.L. 111-5, increased the NMTC allocation for 2008 and 2009 to $5 billion from $3.5 billion. Further, the Tax Relief, Unemployment Insurance

---

* This is an edited, reformatted and augmented version of a Congressional Research Service publication RL34402, prepared for Members and Committees of Congress, dated January 10, 2013.

Reauthorization, and Job Creation Act of 2010 (P.L. 111-312) extended the NMTC authorization through 2011 at $3.5 billion per year. Most recently, the American Taxpayer Relief Act of 2012 (P.L. 112-240) extended the NMTC authorization for 2012 and 2013 at $3.5 billion per year.

OVERVIEW

The New Markets Tax Credit (NMTC) was enacted by the Community Renewal Tax Relief Act of 2000 (P.L. 106-554) to provide an incentive to stimulate investment in low-income communities (LIC). The original allocation authority eligible for the NMTC program was $15 billion from 2001 to 2007.[1] Congress, subsequently, has increased the total allocation authority to $40 billion and extended the program through 2012.[2] Qualified investment groups apply to the U.S. Department of the Treasury's Community Development Financial Institutions Fund (CDFI) for an allocation of the New Markets Tax Credit. The investment group, known as a Community Development Entity (CDE), seeks taxpayers to make qualifying equity investments in the CDE. The CDE then makes equity investments in low-income communities and low-income community businesses, all of which must be qualified. After the CDE is awarded a tax credit allocation, the CDE is authorized to offer the tax credits to private equity investors in the CDE.

The tax credit value is 39% of the cost of the qualified equity investment and is claimed over a seven-year credit allowance period.[3] In each of the first three years of the investment, the investor receives a credit equal to 5% of the total amount paid for the stock or capital interest at the time of purchase. For the final four years, the value of the credit is 6% annually. Investors must retain their interest in a qualified equity investment throughout the seven-year period.

The 112th Congress extended the NMTC program authorization with the American Taxpayer Relief Act of 2012 (P.L. 112-240) through 2012 and 2013 at $3.5 billion per year.

PROGRAM COMPONENTS

The process by which the NMTC affects eligible low-income communities involves multiple agents and steps. *Figure 1* illustrates the key agents in the NMTC process.

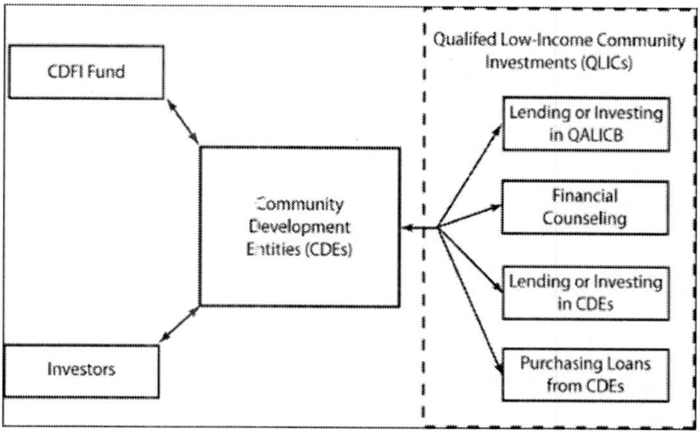

Source: CRS analysis of NMTC program components.

Figure 1. Key Components of the NMTC Process.

The multiple steps and agents are designed to ensure that the tax credit achieves its primary goal: encouraging investment in low-income communities. For example, the Treasury Department's CDFI reviews NMTC applicants submitted by CDEs, issues tax credit authority to those CDEs deemed most qualified, and plays a significant role in program compliance.

Community Development Entities (CDE)

A CDE is a domestic corporation or partnership that is an intermediary vehicle for the provision of loans, investment funding, or financial counseling in low-income communities (LICs). To become certified as a CDE, an organization must submit an application to the CDFI that demonstrates that it meets three criteria: (1) it is a domestic corporation or partnership duly organized under the laws of the jurisdiction in which it is incorporated, (2) it has a primary mission of serving low-income communities, and (3) it maintains accountability to residents of these low-income communities. A CDE may demonstrate meeting the third criterion by filling at least 20% of either its advisory or its governing board positions with representatives of low-income communities.[4]

Only CDEs may apply for the NMTC. Upon receipt of NMTC allocation, CDEs attract investors using the credits. While both for-profit and nonprofit CDEs may apply for the NMTC, only for-profit CDEs may pass the NMTC on to investors. To ensure that projects are selected on economic merit, nonprofit CDEs awarded NMTCs must transfer their allocations to for-profit subsidiaries prior to offering NMTCs to investors.

As *Figure 1* illustrates, CDEs play a critical role in a properly functioning NMTC process. CDEs are the intermediaries between the potential low-income community investments and the CDFI during the application process. CDEs also present investors with investment opportunities and provide the CDFI the majority of its compliance data.

Qualifying Low-Income Communities

Under the tax code's NMTC provisions, only eligible investments in qualifying low-income communities are eligible for the NMTC. Qualifying low-income communities include census tracts that have at least one of the following criteria: (1) a poverty rate of at least 20%; (2) is located in a metropolitan area, a median family income below 80% of the greater of the statewide or metropolitan area median family income; or (3) is located outside a metropolitan area, a median family income below 80% of the median statewide family income. As defined by the criterion above, about 39% of the nation's census tracts covering nearly 36% of the U.S. population are eligible for the NMTC. Additionally, designated targeted populations may be treated as low-income communities.[5] Further, the definition of a low-income community includes census tracts with low populations and census tracts within high migration rural counties. As a result of the definition of qualified low-income communities, virtually all of the country's census tracts are potentially eligible for the NMTC.

Qualified Investors and Investments

All taxable investors are eligible to receive the NMTC. As noted above, investors receiving the credit can claim the NMTC over a seven-year period, starting on the date of the investment and on each anniversary, at a rate of 5% for each of the first three years and a rate of 6% for each of the next four years, for a total of 39%. Once the investor begins claiming the NMTC, the credit can be recaptured if the CDE (1) ceases to be a CDE, (2) fails to use substantially all of the proceeds for eligible purposes, or (3) redeems the investment principal.[6]

Almost all qualified equity investments (QEI) in low-income communities or serving low-income populations could be eligible to receive the NMTC. These eligible investments are referred to as qualified low-income community investments (QLICIs). QLICIs are categorized in four ways: (1) loans or investments to qualified active low-income community businesses (QALICB), (2) the provision of financial counseling, (3) loans or investments in other CDEs, and (4) the purchase of loans from other CDEs.[7] All QLICIs, including QALICBs, are explicitly prohibited from investing in residential rental property and certain types of businesses, such as golf courses and casinos.

NMTC Allocation Process and Compliance

To receive an allocation, a CDE must submit an application to the CDFI, which asks a series of standardized questions about the track record of the CDE, the amount of NMTC allocation authority being requested, and the CDE's plans for any allocation authority granted.

The application covers four areas: (1) the CDE's business strategy to invest in low-income communities, (2) capitalization strategy to raise equity from investors, (3) management capacity, and (4) expected impact on jobs and economic growth in low-income communities where investments are to be made. In addition, priority points are available for addressing the statutory priorities of investing in unrelated entities and having demonstrated a track record of serving disadvantaged businesses or communities. The application is reviewed and scored to identify those applicants most likely to have the greatest community development impact and ranked in descending order of aggregate score.

Tax credit allocations are then awarded based upon the aggregate ranking, until all of the allocation authority is exhausted. In each of the completed NMTC rounds, significantly more CDEs applied for allocations than were able to receive allocations. For example, in the most recent completed allocation round (2011) only 22% of applicants received allocations. Additionally, allocation authority of $26.7 billion was requested, compared with the $3.6 billion in allocation authority available.[8]

Prior to receiving the authority to offer tax credits to investors, every CDE allocatee must sign an allocation agreement. The allocation agreement clarifies the terms and conditions of the allocation authority, such as the total tax credit authority, service areas, authorized uses of the allocation, and CDE reporting requirements. Failing to meet the terms of the allocation agreement subjects the CDE to the potential revocation of allocation authority.

Additionally, the Internal Revenue Service (IRS) monitors compliance with the tax consequences of NMTC allocations, focusing on the "substantially all" requirement.

As specified in the IRS regulations, CDE allocatees must issue tax credits to investors within five years of signing their allocation agreements and invest the QEIs in QLICIs within 12 months of signing their allocation agreements. If these requirements are not satisfied, the CDE loses the authority to allocate the unused NMTC. In addition, CDEs that receive principal payments from their QLICIs have 12 months to reinvest those funds in QLICIs to avoid recapture.

NMTC Investment Activity

Once an allocatee signs its allocation agreement and receives its NMTC allocation authority, it may begin soliciting capital from investors. Column 2 of *Table 1* lists the total allocation awarded to date by the NMTC, by funding round. Investors receive the right to claim NMTCs on a portion of their investment, by acquiring stock or a capital interest in a CDE with an allocation. The CDE, in turn, must invest the proceeds in qualified low-income community investments. Investors have, to date, invested roughly $30.4 billion in CDEs. Columns 3 and 4 list the remaining available NMTC allocation, in dollars and as a percentage, that have not yet been allocated to an investor, by round.

Legislative Developments

Modifications to the NMTC program have been made in each Congress since the NMTC was created. In the 108th Congress, the American Jobs Creation Act of 2004 (P.L. 108-357, 118 Stat. 1418) included provisions expanding the authority of the Secretary of the Treasury to treat certain other tracts and targeted populations as low-income communities.[9]

During the 109th Congress, the Gulf Opportunity Zone Act of 2005 (P.L. 109-135, 119 Stat. 2577) was enacted to provide tax relief to businesses and individuals affected by Hurricanes Katrina, Wilma, and Rita.

Table 1. NMTC Qualified Equity Investment, by Allocation Round

Allocation Round (Year)	Total Allocation	Remaining Available Allocation	Percent Remaining
Round 1 (2001-2002)	$2,485,699,042.00	$0.13	0.00%
Round 2 (2003-2004)	$3,493,786,205.00	$0.71	0.00%
Round 3 (2005)	$1,964,830,000.00	$141,144.40	0.01%
Round 4 (2006)	$4,099,765,000.00	$0.00	0.00%
Round 5 (2007)	$3,893,000,000.00	$36,750,979.52	0.94%
Round 6 (2008)	$4,965,000,000.00	$173,127,744.05	3.49%
Round 7 (2009)	$5,000,000,000.00	$405,846,901.83	8.12%
Round 8 (2010)	$3,475,000,000.00	$507,368,132.17	14.60%
Round 9 (2011)	$3,622,919,753.00	$1,501,590,047.32	41.45%
Totala	$33,000,000,000.00	$2,624,824,950.13	7.95%

Source: CRS analysis of NMTC Qualified Equity Investment Report (December 3, 2012). a. Columns may not sum to total due to rounding.

The bill, which created the Gulf Opportunity Zone (or GO Zone), provided an additional $1 billion in allocation authority to CDEs with a significant mission in the recovery and redevelopment of low-income communities in the Katrina GO Zone.[10]

Also during the 109th Congress, the Tax Relief and Health Care Act of 2006 (P.L. 109-432, 120 Stat. 2922) extended the NMTC for one year, through 2008, with an additional allocation of $3.5 billion and mandated Treasury to promulgate regulations to ensure that non-metropolitan counties receive a proportional allocation of investments under the NMTC.

In the 110th Congress, legislative attention focused primarily on extending the NMTC program authorization. This attention came to fruition with the enactment of P.L. 110-343, which extended the NMTC program authorization one year, through the end of 2009. This one-year extension was also proposed in H.R. 6049, S. 2886, S. 3098, and H.R. 7060. In addition, H.R. 2075 and S. 1239 proposed to extend the NMTC through 2013 and would have authorized allocations of $3.5 billion, indexed for inflation, for each of the years. Also introduced during the 110th Congress, H.R. 3907 proposed to make the NMTC permanent.

In the 111th Congress, the American Recovery and Reinvestment Tax Act of 2009 P.L. 111-5 increased the NMTC allocation for 2008 and 2009, to $5 billion from $3.5 billion. For the additional 2008 allocation, the CDFI Fund distributes the additional $1.5 billion in NMTCs to applicants of the original 2008 allocation round.

Also in the 111th Congress, the Tax Relief, Unemployment Insurance Reauthorization, and Job Creation Act of 2010 (P.L. 111-312) extended the NMTC authorization through 2011 at $3.5 billion per year.

In the 112th Congress the American Taxpayer Relief Act of 2012 (P.L. 112-240) extended the NMTC authorization for 2012 and 2013 at $3.5 billion per year.

POLICY CONSIDERATIONS

The New Markets Tax Credit Program is set to expire at the end of 2013. As Congress debates reauthorization of the NMTC, the following policy considerations could be pertinent to any consideration of these bills.

The NMTC is primarily intended to encourage private capital investment in eligible low-income communities. However, the source of the investment funds has implications for the effectiveness of the program in achieving its objective. From an economic perspective, the impact of the NMTC would be greatest in the case where the investment represents new investment in the U.S. economy that would not have occurred in the absence of the program. Conversely, the impact of the NMTC is diminished to the extent the tax credit is applied to investment that would have otherwise occurred or been funded by a shift in investment from more productive alternatives.[11]

To date, only one study has empirically assessed the question of whether NMTC investment is funded through shifted investment or whether it represents new investment.[12] The findings of the study suggest that corporate investment represented a shift in investment location. In contrast, the authors concluded that a portion of individual NMTC investment, roughly $641 million, represented new investment.

Although important, understanding the source of NMTC investments alone is not sufficient to determine the effectiveness of the NMTC. A comprehensive review of the program would require an accounting of both the social and economic costs and benefits of the NMTC, an undertaking which may pose considerable challenges. For example, this would include examining the efficiency and opportunity costs of the NMTC investments, while a comprehensive accounting of the NMTC benefits would need to identify and value "spillovers" such as its effect on neighboring businesses and communities. The CDFI Fund is working with a contractor on a comprehensive review of the NMTC, which may include an assessment of the effectiveness of the NMTC.

Others, notably GAO, have recommended that the NMTC be simplified by converting the NMTC into a grant program.[13] This option may be able to deliver the same level of incentive with lower cost to the government, as investors do not generally "buy" tax credits at face value—allowing a smaller grant to provide a similar level of incentive. Specifically, tax credit markets historically set a price of 70 to 80 cents per dollar of tax credit, with lower valuations in recent years due to tight credit markets and decreased corporate profits.

A grant option, however, likely provides a lesser incentive for investors to invest in NMTC projects, as they may not be the beneficiary of the incentive.[14] If this occurs, improving the access to capital in low-income communities (an NMTC program goal) would be more difficult. Further, a grant program may complicate existing mechanisms designed to ensure the NMTC is used for intended purposes, as CDEs are likely less capitalized than investors and the possible removal of IRS authority to recapture benefits (as the NMTC would no longer be a tax program).

An additional issue is the geographic distribution of NMTC activity. Initial concerns focused on distinctions between urban and rural NMTC activity and have been addressed through legislation. Further, NMTC activity has occurred in all 50 states, the District of Columbia, and Puerto Rico. However, the distribution of NMTC activity appears concentrated in a few states—with the nine states with the highest activity accounting for over 50% of all NMTC activity.[15] In contrast, the 25 states with the least NMTC activity account for less than 10% of all NMTC activity. The current distribution of activity is not likely to reflect the distribution of low-income populations and may raise questions concerning the equity of the NMTC.

Finally, the NMTC is one of several programs designed to improve conditions in low-income communities. In a 2004 assessment of the NMTC, the Office of Management and Budget noted that the goal of the NMTC overlaps that of several other tax credits and numerous programs administered by the Departments of Housing and Urban Development and Commerce.[16] Given this overlap and the desire to target federal funds to their most productive uses, it follows that information on the performance of the NMTC relative to other programs with a similar goal would be of use. To date, however, no comparative, empirical study of this nature has been undertaken.

End Notes

[1] Congress provided a schedule limiting the NMTC allocation authority for calendar years 2001 through 2007. The schedule allowed for $1.0 billion in allocation authority in 2001, $1.5 billion in 2002 and 2003, $2.0 billion in 2004 and 2005, and $3.5 billion in 2006 and 2007.

[2] The Gulf Opportunity Zone Act of 2005 (P.L. 109-135) authorized an additional $1 billion of NMTC equity for qualified investments in areas affected by Hurricane Katrina, the Tax Relief and Health Care Act of 2006 (P.L. 109- 432) extended the NMTC for an additional year (through 2008) with an additional $3.5 billion of NMTC allocation authority, and the Emergency Economic Stabilization Act of 2008 (P.L. 110-343) extended the NMTC for an additional year (through 2009) with an additional $3.5 billion of NMTC allocation authority. In the 111th Congress, the American Recovery and Reinvestment Tax Act of 2009, P.L. 111-5, increased the NMTC allocation for 2008 and 2009, to $5 billion from $3.5 billion and the Tax Relief, Unemployment Insurance Reauthorization, and Job Creation Act of 2010 (P.L. 111-312) extended the NMTC authorization through 2011 at $3.5 billion per year. In the 112th Congress the American Taxpayer Relief Act of 2012 (P.L. 112-240) extended the NMTC authorization for 2012 and 2013 at $3.5 billion per year.

[3] In present value terms, the credit is equal to approximately 30% of the eligible investment at a 6.7% discount rate.

[4] In addition, all Community Development Financial Institutions or Specialized Small Business Investment Companies automatically qualify as CDEs. To be recognized as CDEs, these entities are required to register through the CDFI Fund website.

[5] See Internal Revenue Bulletin 2006-29, Notice 2006-60, issued July 17, 2006, for a more complete description of the definition of designated targeted populations.

[6] According to IRS regulations, the "substantially all" requirement is met if at least 85% of investor proceeds are used to make eligible investments in the first six years of the NMTC period and at least 75% in year seven of the investment.

[7] For a business to be a QALICB, it must be located in a qualifying census tract, derive at least 50% of gross income from activity conducted in a LIC, have at least 40% of both the use of tangible property and services provided located or performed in the LIC, and have less than 5% of the aggregate unadjusted bases of the property attributable to collectibles or non-qualified financial property.

[8] Community Development Financial Institutions Fund, 2011 New Markets Tax Credit Program Allocations, Washington, DC, 2012, http://www.cdfifund.gov/docs/2011/nmtc/2011%20NMTC%20Award%20Book.pdf.

[9]The term "targeted population," as defined in 12 U.S.C. 4702(20), means individuals, or an identifiable group of individuals, including an Indian tribe, who (1) are low-income persons (low-income targeted population) or (2) otherwise lack adequate access to loans or equity investments.

[10] The Gulf Opportunity Zone (GO ZONE) is defined as those areas in Alabama, Mississippi, and Louisiana that have been designated by the federal government as warranting assistance due to Hurricane Katrina. Disaster areas associated with hurricanes Rita and Wilma are not eligible for the additional allocation.

[11] However, from a policy perspective, the desire to minimize the distortion of investment choice caused by the NMTC is usually balanced against other objectives, such as equity.

[12] Tami Gurley-Calvez et al., "Do tax incentives affect investment? An analysis of the New Markets Tax Credit," Public Finance Review, vol. 34, no. 4, pp. 371-398.

[13] U.S. Government Accountability Office, New Markets Tax Credit: The Credit Helps Fund a Variety of Projects on Low-Income Communities, but Could be Simplified, GAO-10-334, January 29, 2011, http://www.gao.gov/products/ GAO-10-334.

[14] Allowing CDEs to assign the grants to specific investors is an option to mitigate this problem.

[15] These figures are based upon CRS analysis of CDFI Fund data on investments though FY2010. The data are available at http://www.cdfifund.gov/docs/2011/nmtc/NMTC%20Projects%20 Through%202010%20REVISED-2.xls.

[16] See U.S. Office of Management and Budget, Detailed Information on the New Markets Tax Credit Assessment, updated January 29, 2008, http://www.whitehouse.gov/omb/ expectmore/detail/10002230.2004.html.

In: The New Markets Tax Credit
Editor: Marlin Barrett

ISBN: 978-1-63463-644-5

Chapter 2

NEW MARKETS TAX CREDITS: UNLOCKING INVESTMENT POTENTIAL*

David Black

ABSTRACT

This *Insights* report describes the New Markets Tax Credit (NMTC) Program and the major considerations banks may need to address when using the tax credits to support community and economic development activities. The report examines the primary opportunities and risks associated with the use of NMTCs and discusses the methods used by national banks and federal savings associations (collectively, banks) to structure transactions and use the credits effectively. The report addresses banks' participation in the NMTC Program as investors, as recipients of the tax credits (allocatees), and as leverage lenders.

The information in this report was obtained from a variety of sources, including banks, nonsupervised financial intermediaries, investment fund advisers, and others that actively use NMTCs to finance a diverse range of activities. This information represents our understanding of federal income tax laws and regulations but does not constitute tax advice. Banks should consult their tax advisers about the tax treatments described in this report and the consequences that may apply to their own transactions.

---

* This is an edited, reformatted and augmented version of a Community Development Insights report issued by the Office of the Comptroller of the Currency, June 2013.

Project summaries of several NMTC transactions are included in a case study in appendix A. Appendix B presents a glossary of terms about the NMTC Program. The resource directory in appendix C contains sources of additional information on the program.

I. What Is the New Markets Tax Credit Program?

The NMTC Program was created in December 2000 by the Community Renewal Tax Relief Act of 2000.[1] The program is jointly administered by the Community Development Financial Institutions Fund (CDFI Fund) and the Internal Revenue Service (IRS).[2] The NMTC Program uses federal tax incentives to attract private capital into operating businesses and real estate in urban and rural low-income communities (LIC). Through May 2013, the CDFI Fund had awarded approximately $36.5 billion in NMTC authority to specially designated financial institutions called community development entities (CDE).[3] The CDEs use those credits to raise private capital, which is then invested in qualifying projects.

From 2003 through 2009, $6 billion in NMTC credits generated nearly $50 billion in financing to businesses and commercial real estate projects in low-income communities. [4] The tax credit helped fund a variety of qualified businesses, including commercial and industrial facilities, retail and mixed-use projects, community facilities, "green" energy-producing facilities, and equipment and working capital for operating businesses. According to a 2008 study, more than 75 percent of NMTC-financed projects were in communities with significant levels of distress .[5]

By investing in a CDE with an NMTC allocation, an investor is able to claim a federal tax credit equal to 39 percent of the investment, which is referred to as a qualified equity investment (QEI).[6] The tax credit is claimed over a seven-year period, with 5 percent of the investment amount claimed in each of the first three years and 6 percent in each of the following four years, as shown below. The NMTC Program provides a relatively "shallow" subsidy into the projects: NMTCs amount to approximately 20 percent to 30 percent' of the total project costs?' In the standard NMTC structure, the investor receiving the tax credit typically recovers all or a portion of the original investment after the end of the seven-year compliance period.

The investor may also receive additional economic benefits, such as interest payments, from the investment.

Table 1. Schedule of Tax Credit Benefits for a $10 Million QEI

Year 1	$500,000	5%
2	$500,000	5
3	$500,000	6
4	$600,000	5
5	$600,000	6
6	$600,000	6
7	$600,000	6
Total	$3,900,000	39%

Source: OCC.

Banks can participate in the NMTC Program in several ways Banks can be allocatees, receiving NMTC allocation authority from the CDFI Fund through bank-owned CDEs. Through the 2011 funding round, bank-controlled CDEs have received approximately 23 percent of the NMTC allocations from the CDFI Fund. Banks can also be investors, either in their own CDEs or in third-party CDEs. In 2011, 86 percent of the money invested in CDEs came from regulated depository institutions.[9] Banks can be lenders, providing loans into the leverage structure investments described later in this report. In practice, banks play significant roles in the NMTC Program and can participate in multiple ways on a single project.

II. Why Is the NMTC Program of Interest to Banks?

NMTCs are of interest to banks for the following reasons.

NMTCs are a critical tool in helping meet the credit needs of low-income communities. According to program guidelines, an NMTC investment must be made in a low-income community[10] or serve a targeted population.[11] In practice, most of the investments go to areas of higher distress than required by the regulations.[12] The tax credits bring new private investment into poor communities. According to the U.S. Government Accountability Office (GAO), 88 percent of the NMTC investors surveyed said they would not have invested in a low-income community without the tax credit.[13] NMTCs have helped banks support needed community facilities, such as charter schools[14] and grocery stores.[15]

Community impact and accountability are essential to the NMTC Program. CDE applicants to the program must demonstrate the ability to

- identify investments in low-income communities or that serve target populations.
- achieve selected community development outcomes.
- track projected outcomes.
- meaningfully engage community stakeholders around planned NMTC investments.
- finance activities that encourage other non-NMTC investments in their low-income communities.

NMTCs are important in helping meet customer needs. NMTCs provide resources that can help create a satisfactory loan structure for a customer who might otherwise be turned down or offered a loan at a much higher rate. The tax credit provides a subsidy that is used to substantially reduce the interest rate on loans to businesses[16] or to enhance the business owner's equity in a transaction by leaving a portion of the investment in the project after the NMTC compliance period, as described later in this report. In addition, NMTC loans to qualifying businesses often have flexible terms, including lower origination fees, extended interest-only payment periods, higher loan-to-value (LTV) ratios, lower debt coverage ratios (DCR), and longer amortization periods.

NMTCs can be used in connection with many other credit enhancements that support development in low-income communities. These enhancements include historic rehabilitation tax credits, renewable-energy investment tax credits,[17] state NMTCs, and several U.S. Department of Agriculture (USDA) loan programs.[18]

NMTCs can help banks meet their financial goals. Investors in NMTCs can receive competitive returns on their equity investments. Leverage lenders may earn rates at or near market rates and are able to participate in transactions that would not be feasible without NMTCs.

NMTCs can help banks meet their Community Reinvestment Act (CRA) requirements.[19] A bank can receive consideration for its investments in CDEs, or for the pro rata portion of a loan originated by a CDE, based on the bank's percentage of equity ownership in the CDE. A bank can also receive a partial credit for the investment and a partial credit for the loan. The investment in the CDE must benefit a bank's assessment area or a broader state or regional area that includes its assessment area.[20] In the case of leverage structure transactions,[21] the equity investor and the leverage lender each may receive CRA consideration based on the pro rata share of their investment.

III. HOW DOES THE NMTC PROGRAM WORK?

CDEs are specially designated financial institutions that receive allocations of NMTCs from the CDFI Fund, use those credits to raise QEIs from investors, and then invest the QEI proceeds into qualified low-income community investments (QLICI).[22] Figure 1 shows how the program works.

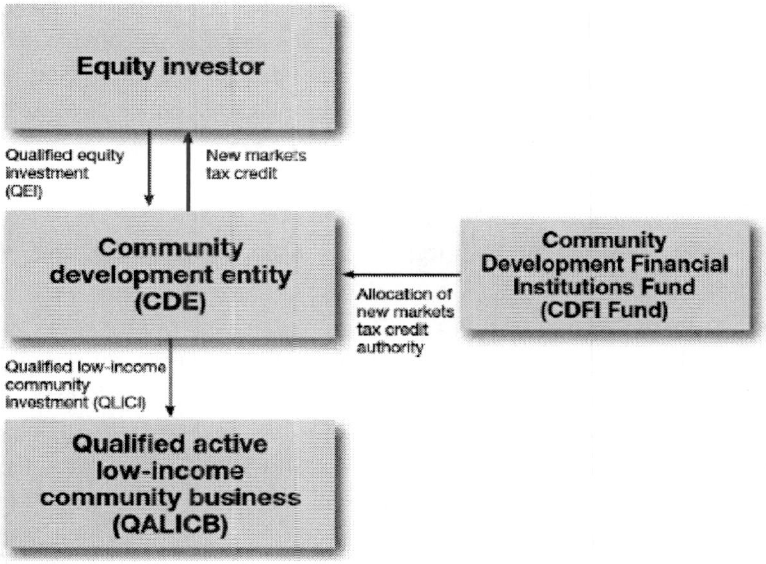

Source: OCC.

Figure 1. New Markets Tax Credit Program: Key Terms and Relationships.

A CDE is formally defined' as a domestic corporation or partnership that

- has a primary mission of serving or providing investment capital for low-income communities or individuals,
- maintains accountability to residents of low-income communities through the residents' representation on a governing board or advisory board of the CDE, and
- has been certified as a CDE by the CDFI Fund.

Specialised Small Business Investment Companies (SBIC)[24] certified by the Small Business Administration CDFIs' certified by the CDFI Fund automatically qualify for CDE certification.' Affiliates of CDFIs and SBICs do not automatically qualify as CDEs and must complete the certification process.

Nonprofit and for-profit entities may apply for CDE certification. All CDEs are eligible to receive loans and investments from, or sell loans to, other CDEs that have been issued tax credit allocations by the CDFI Fund. Only for-profit CDEs, however, may raise capital by offering tax credits to investors. A nonprofit CDE applying for an NMTC allocation must present a strategy to form and transfer its entire allocation to a for-profit subsidiary or subsidiaries.

Awards of NMTC allocation authority from the CDFI Fund have been very competitive. Since the program's inception, the CDFI Fund has made 749 allocation awards totaling $36.5 billion.[27] Demand for the credits has far exceeded the supply. In 2011, 314 CDEs requested $26.7 billion from a pool of $3.6 billion in allocation authority.[28] Successful CDE applicants must show, among other criteria, that they can

- identify investment opportunities in distressed areas.
- offer flexible or non-traditional financial products that meet community needs.
- raise capital from investors.
- deploy that capital within three years of the allocation.
- manage those investments and comply with NMTC regulations.

With an allocation of NMTCs from the CDFI Fund, a CDE allocatee can then raise equity from investors. The investments, or QEIs, are usually in the form of stock purchases if the CDE is a corporation or an equity investment in a limited partnership interest if the CDE is a partnership. A CDE must place the credits with investors within five years of receiving the allocation. As of February 2013, there was approximately $1.9 billion in uncommitted NMTCs.[29] QEIs totaled $3.8 billion in 2009, $4.2 billion in 2010, and $5.7 billion in 2011.[30]

"Substantially all,"[31] or at least 85 percent, of the investment in a CDE must be used within one year for QLICIs.[32] Eligible investments include

- loans or investments into qualified active low-income community businesses (QALICB).
- loans or investments into other CDEs that, in turn, make QLICIs.

- loans purchased from other CDEs, if the loan is a QLICI.
- financial counseling or other services to businesses in or residents of low-income communities.

A QALICB can be

- an operating business in a low-income community.
- a business that develops or rehabilitates commercial, industrial, retail, and mixed-use real estate projects in a low-income community.
- a business that develops or rehabilitates community facilities such as charter schools or health centers in a low-income community.[33]
- a business that develops or rehabilitates for-sale housing in a low-income community.

Examples include for-profit retail businesses, mixed-use shopping centers, manufacturers, service providers, community facilities, and nonprofit businesses. Qualifying businesses must meet several eligibility requirements. Rental housing and certain types of businesses (including golf courses, racetracks, gambling facilities, and massage parlors) are specifically excluded.[34]

In 2006, Congress required the NMTC Program to ensure that nonmetropolitan counties receive proportional allocation of QEIs.[35] To implement this, the CDFI Fund established a process so that a proportionate number of applicants that are "rural CDEs" receive tax credits, and that at least 20 percent of the proposed aggregate investments made with each round of NMTC allocations are made in eligible nonmetropolitan counties.[36]

Most NMTC investments are structured in one of two ways: the standard structure or the leverage structure.

Standard Transactions

In a standard transaction, the NMTC is typically used to reduce the interest rate on the loan to the borrower (QALICB) below what the market would otherwise dictate. The transaction is structured as follows: An investor makes a QEI into a CDE (often through a sub-CDE created as a single-transaction entity), and the CDE then makes a QLICI (almost always a loan) to an eligible project (QALICB). The investor receives two cash streams over the seven-year compliance period: the interest payments on the loan to the QALICB, passed through the CDE, and the tax credits the investor claims on federal tax returns. The tax credit allows the CDE to offer the QALICB a considerable reduction in interest rates, while allowing the investor to receive market rate returns on the investment. Figure 2 shows how the standard transaction works.

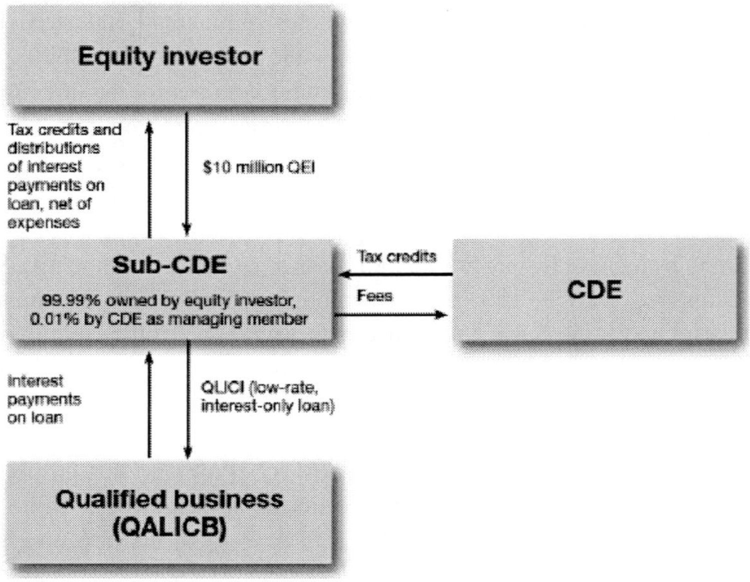

Source: OCC.

Figure 2. NMTC Standard Transaction.

For example, consider the benefit stream going back to an investor from a $10 million QLICI made by a CDE (figure 2 and scenario B of table 2). Using the standard transaction structure, the investor receives a tax credit of 39 percent on the $10 million, or $3.9 million. This works out to an annual rate of return to the investor of approximately 5.6 percent as a result of the credits alone.

If the investor wants to receive a rate of return equivalent to the market rate (in this example, 8 percent), the CDE could drop the interest rate to the borrower (QALICB) to as low as 2.4 percent.' And while the investor receives a market return, the borrower, with a 2.4 percent loan, saves $3.9 million in interest expense over the course of the seven-year compliance period.' With this structure, the investor expects either to recover all of its initial investment at the end of the compliance period or to convert its investment in the CDE into a conventional loan to the QALICB.

Table 2. Comparative Distribution of NMTC Benefits

CDE loan to QALICB	Scenario A: Market rate loan (no NMTCs) $10 million loan	Scenario B: NMTC standard transaction $10 million loan	Scenario C: NMTC leverage structure transaction $10 million loan in A-note and B-note
Interest rate	8%	2.4%	8% (A-note) 1% (B-note)
Interest revenue	$5,600,000	$1,700,020	$4,502,400
Tax credits	$0	$3,900,000	$3,900,000
Total financial benefit	$5,600,000	$5,600,020	$8,402,400
Net benefit after put/call $2,800,000	Not applicable	Not applicable	$5,602,400
Borrower cost: interest payments	$5,600,000	$1,700,000	$4,502,400
Borrower savings			
Interest expense	$0	$3,899,980	$1,097,600
Equity	$0	$0	$2,800,000
Effective subsidy	$0	$3,899,980	$3,897,600

Source: OCC.

Banks have used this structure to offer low-interest loans to qualifying customers. In some cases, banks have developed standardized paperwork and processes to minimize NMTC transaction costs. This allows the banks to use the NMTC with smaller transactions than allowed by the leverage structure described below. With a steady stream of customers demanding smaller transactions, CDEs can more easily redeploy any funds repaid during the seven-year compliance period to other borrowers and avoid any violations of the "substantially all" requirement.[39] The CDE can receive principal repayments during the compliance period and the money can be re-lent to additional borrowers relatively quickly and efficiently. This ability to make loans for shorter terms and lower amounts makes the standard transaction model particularly attractive for lending to operating businesses.

Leverage Structure Transactions

Under the leverage structure, the NMTCs are used to leverage additional investment into a project. The leverage structure can offer more attractive returns to investors than the standard structure, attracting more capital to the program. The leverage structure also benefits the QALICB differently than the standard transaction structure. Typically, a portion of the investor's equity is sold to the QALICB for a nominal price at the end of the seven-year compliance period rather than being returned to the investor. This boost in the owner's equity allows for greater access to conventional financing at standard LTV ratios.

NMTC investments using the leverage structure differ from those using the standard structure.[40] (See figure 3.) In the leverage structure, the equity investor borrows from a leverage lender, blends those borrowed funds with its own cash, and then uses the blended funds to make a QEI into a CDE (again, typically through a sub-CDE created as a single-transaction entity). Typically, the equity investor receives tax credits on the full amount of the QEI, and the leverage lender receives interest on the amount borrowed by the equity investor.[41]

To execute a leverage structure transaction, the equity investor forms a wholly owned limited liability entity called an Investment Fund. The equity investor capitalizes the Investment Fund with an amount of cash equivalent to the present value of the stream of tax credits that will be generated by the investment. Industry practitioners reported that the investor's contribution is typically 25 percent to 28 percent of the total amount of the QEI that will go into the CDE.[42] The leverage lender makes a nonrecourse loan to the Investment Fund.

The borrowed funds and the equity investor's cash are pooled in the Investment Fund and used to make a QEI into a CDE. The CDE then makes a QLICI into a QALICB. The CDE may make two loans into the QALICB: an A-note in the amount of the leverage lender's debt contribution to the Investment Fund, and a B-note at below-market rates equal to the amount of the equity investor's contribution less any fees retained by the CDE.

The CDE passes the tax credits and interest earned on the investment (less any fees) back to the Investment Fund, where they are distributed to the equity investor and leverage lender. The equity investor receives the full amount of tax credits generated by the pooled investment. This substantially increases the return the equity investor receives on its equity contribution. The leverage lender receives interest-only payments on the leverage loan throughout the seven-year compliance period. The interest rate earned by the leverage lender can be at or near market rates.

The equity investor normally receives a sufficient return on its investment from tax credits alone. NMTC leverage structure agreements typically allow the QALICB or an affiliate of the QALICB to purchase the investor's interest in the Investment Fund through a "put/call" technique[43] that generates a subsidy or grant equivalent in the amount of the B-note less the negotiated purchase price. The QALICB or affiliate then repays or renegotiates the A-note with the leverage lender. A key assumption behind this structure is that after seven years of operation the QALICB will be a stronger credit, particularly with the improved LTV ratio as a result of the N1VITC equity being absorbed into the project.

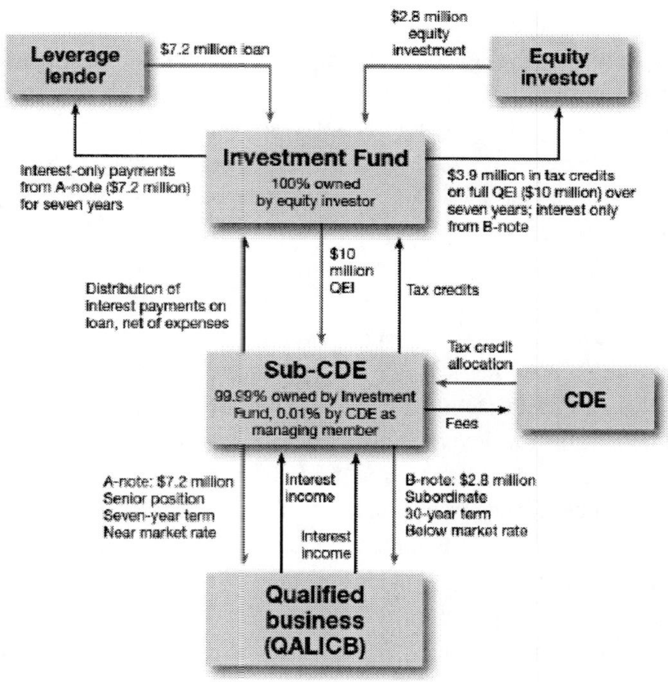

Source: OCC.

Figure 3. NMTC Leverage Structure Transaction.

Returning to table 1, in scenario C we can see how the returns to investors and benefits to the QALICB differ in the leverage structure. The $10 million QEI is made up of $2.8 million in investor equity and a $7.2 million leverage loan. Because the investor receives tax credits on the entire QEI (39 percent of $10 million, or $3,900,000), the return to the investor is increased to 9 percent, a substantial increase when compared with the 6 percent return earned under the standard transaction model.

In this example, the investor also receives 1 percent interest from the B-note,' and the leverage lender receives an 8 percent interest-only rate on its loan of $7.2 million. Together, the equity investor and the leverage lender receive $8 4 million in interest expense and tax benefits, considerably more than the $5.6 million received through either the market transaction or standard transaction scenarios. Because it is expected, however, that the QALICB will purchase the equity investor's interest in the Investment Fund for a nominal fee, in the leverage structure scenario the return is discounted by $2.8 million, the amount of the equity investor's interest in the Investment Fund.

The borrower in the leverage structure still benefits from a lower interest rate on its loan from the CDE (a 6.43 percent blended rate[45] on the entire $10 million loan), although the discount is not as steep as in the standard transaction model. In the leverage structure, the QALICB realizes a benefit from the equity left in the project at the end of the compliance period, as well as savings in interest. As can be seen in the "borrower savings" section of table 1, the amount of subsidy in the leverage structure remains the same as in the standard or subsidized interest rate model, but the subsidy is deployed differently.

Lenders are attracted to the NMTC leverage structure because it helps them make loans at or near market rates with a more favorable LTV ratio. The leverage structure is attractive to equity investors because the returns they achieve when using the leverage structure are much higher than they would achieve using the standard transaction model. The return for investors increases from approximately 5 percent to 6 percent in the standard model to 9 percent to 10 percent in the leverage structure, depending in part on how much the equity investor pays for the credits. In addition, the risks for the equity investor are more limited in the leverage structure than they are in the standard model because the equity investor in a leverage transaction does not need to recover its initial investment in order to achieve a financial return.

Several examples of leverage structure transactions are illustrated in appendix A. Banks can use the leverage structure to strengthen loans to customers. Project sponsors can use the attractive rates of return offered with the leverage structure to attract equity investors that might not normally participate in a community development project. Traditionally, banks have been the principal source of leverage loans to NMTC transactions.

Increasingly, new sources of hard and soft debt, such as debt from public and philanthropic sources, have been used in leverage transactions. Moreover, multiple banks and other entities can participate on both the debt and equity sides to bring transactions to scale.

The leverage structure is not appropriate for all circumstances. This structure raises the complexity and therefore the costs of the transaction. Some industry experts have suggested a minimum size for a leverage transaction of about $5 million to $10 million to justify the higher transaction costs. The leverage structure is generally less appropriate when the interest rate on the loan needs to be well below market, for example, when the DCR is more important than the LTV ratio. With smaller transactions, or deals in which fees and transaction costs need to be minimized, alternative NMTC structures should be considered.

Multiple-CDE Transactions

Larger NMTC projects can involve multiple CDEs. Each of the contributing CDEs provides a portion of the equity in a transaction, limiting each CDE's exposure and allowing it to participate in larger transactions than it could individually. Multiple-CDE transactions can be more expensive, because each CDE must expend transaction fees for due diligence, document preparation, closing costs, ongoing asset management and audit fees, and closing costs at the end of the compliance period. CDEs participating in these types of transactions have begun to explore cost-sharing arrangements to reduce duplicative efforts and make the transactions more efficient.

Twinning

Commercial real estate projects that combine federal NMTCs with state NMTCs,[46] historic rehabilitation tax credits[47] (HTC), or renewable-energy investment tax credits[48] (ITC)—often referred to as "twinned" transactions—have been popular with some bank investors, because the blend of NMTC and HTC or ITC equity increases the return for investors in these projects and enables transactions that previously were considered unattractive to be financed.[49]

IV. What Are the Key Risks and Regulatory Issues Associated With the NMTC Program?

The risks a bank may face in an NMTC transaction depend in part on its role in the transaction. Bank investors in NMTCs are concerned with acquiring and using the credits over the seven-year compliance period. Both investors and allocatees want to avoid recapture of the credits by ensuring compliance with program requirements. Leverage lenders want their loans repaid and face challenges that often differ from those presented by conventional financing. And, regardless of role, banks have accounting and regulatory issues to consider.

Key Risks

Recapture Risk

Under the NMTC Program, tax credits can be recaptured if

- the CDE ceases to be a CDF, Fund-certified CDE,
- "substantially all"[50] of the QEI proceeds are no longer continuously invested in QLICIs, or
- the CDE redeems[51] the equity investment.

Generally, if the transaction is structured properly and compliance is up to date, the risk of recapture is low.

The penalties for recapture are severe, however, when compared with other types of community development tax credits. When the recapture provisions are triggered at any point during the seven-year compliance period, 100 percent of the credits are recaptured, along with interest and penalties, for the entire period. Because the tax credit investor's financial return comes primarily from the tax credits, recapture has significant negative consequences.

A CDE's designation as a CDE lasts for the life of the organization, provided the CDE continues to comply with NMTC Program requirements. To maintain its status as a CDE, the CDE must demonstrate that at least 60 percent of its products and services are directed toward serving low-income communities or individuals and that at least 20 percent of its governing or advisory board members are representatives of a low-income community within the CDE's service area. A CDE may be required, on an annual basis, to certify to the CDFI Fund that it continues to meet its primary mission and accountability requirements. A CDE with NMTC allocations (from the CDFI Fund or another CDE) may be required to provide additional reports.[52] NMTC investors are generally advised to check annually that a CDE is fulfilling its accountability requirements.

CDEs are required to have "substantially all" of the QEI proceeds invested in QLICIs. CDEs must invest the proceeds of a QEI within one year, and fees cannot exceed 15 percent of the QEI. Violations of the "substantially all" test may occur after the initial QLICI investments have been made if a CDE is making QLICIs of less than seven-year maturities, if a QALICB is in a foreclosure situation, or if the CDE steps in as owner of a QALICB. CDEs have 12 months to reinvest any QLICIs that are repaid or recovered. CDEs that are at risk of not meeting the "substantially all" test should develop a pipeline of additional QLICI opportunities.[53] CDEs with QALICBs facing foreclosure should thoroughly understand the responsibilities and options of a CDE in this situation.

A QEI cannot be redeemed during the seven-year compliance period. Generally, QLICIs are not amortized because the payments cannot be passed upstream to the investor and "substantially all" of the QEI must be invested in QLICIs throughout the compliance period. When there is a recovery of nonaccruing funds, however, and in certain circumstances in which credits are twinned, additional scrutiny may be necessary to avoid redemption.

Industry practitioners advise that the strength of the CDE is a key factor in the decision to invest in an NMTC project. The investor is entering into a seven-year relationship with the CDE, and it is important that the CDE have the capacity and expertise to manage the investment throughout the compliance period. The investor often wants to see that the CDE has a track record of successfully developing and managing NMTC investments. The CDE also needs to have the systems in place to assure that it meets the requirements of a CDE and that "substantially all" of the proceeds of the QEI are invested in QLICIs.

Default Risk

Allocatees, investors, and lenders all have strong incentives to see NMTC projects thrive. Standard-structure investors and leverage lenders both expect to receive interest income over the seven-year compliance program, as well as the repayment or refinancing of their initial investment. Because leverage structure investors derive most or all of their financial return on the NMTC investment from the tax credits, and the tax credits will continue even if the project goes into bankruptcy, they may be seen as having less risk. However, recovery of all or a portion of the original QLICI puts the investment at risk with the "substantially all" test, which may lead to recapture if not properly reinvested within 12 months of recovery.

Nonpayment risk can be mitigated with sound underwriting of both the CDE and the QALICB. Investors and lenders should look for a CDE with a strong track record in NMTC or similar types of investments. The CDE should have proven capabilities in identifying and underwriting NMTC-like investments, asset and risk management, NMTC compliance, and raising equity and market rate lending capital. The CDE should be financially sustainable throughout the seven-year compliance period and subsequent unwinding of the transactions. The CDE should also have a pipeline of qualifying projects and suitable underwriting and advisory procedures to reasonably ensure that the projects are consistent with community needs and priorities.

Leverage loans are underwritten and risk-rated according to traditional underwriting standards. Bank leverage loans are often underwritten by specialized lending departments (i.e., retail, institutional, or commercial real estate) rather than the community development departments where NMTC programs are commonly located.

Leverage lenders have challenges that differ from those raised by conventional financing. Because the collateral on the loan is held by the CDE, the leverage lender has only an indirect security on the loan. To avoid triggering the recapture provision if "substantially all" of the QEI does not stay invested during the entire seven-year compliance period, leverage lenders are typically bound by standstill agreements that permit the lender to collect only interest during the seven-year compliance period. Additionally, forbearance agreements restrict the ability of the leverage lender to foreclose during the compliance period. If the CDE does foreclose on a QALICB, the proceeds are usually reinvested in another project.

Most bank leverage lenders interviewed reported few material concerns with these requirements, although some also referred to the use of "work-around" procedures to mitigate the effects of these requirements. For example, the lack of amortization during the seven-year compliance period could be a concern. Some banks described using sinking funds, with the borrower depositing any excess cash after expenses into a reserve, as a way to mitigate the lack of amortization. After the compliance period ends, the proceeds of the sinking fund are then used to retire the principal in a lump sum.

In the case of foreclosure and redeployment, funds must be redeployed within 12 months of the cash being returned to the CDE. Because the process of foreclosure starts well before the return of funds, this gives the partners adequate time to find another transaction. The leverage lender may negotiate a time period (usually six months) to find and suggest a new project that meets their needs and credit standards. The leverage lender may also require specific underwriting standards (i.e., LTV or DCR) for a period. Eventually, however, all of the restrictions imposed by the lender expire, and the CDE can make a decision unilaterally to invest in another project before the deadline triggering recapture.

Reputational Risk

Banks also need to consider reputational risk. The NMTC Program was created to meet the public goals of revitalizing low-income communities and assisting low-income individuals. Banks participating in NMTC transactions need to consider how these public goals are being met, how the community supports the project being financed, and how the benefits to low-income communities and individuals are documented. CDEs may ask a QALICB to sign a Community Benefits Agreement that outlines the goals of the project and details responsibilities for tracking community impact, including jobs and the provision of community services. Failure to adequately identify and document community support and community impact may violate allocation agreements[54] with the CDFI Fund, and could result in negative publicity on the use of public funds.

Liquidity Risk

Because no mature secondary market exists for these investments, NMTCs are highly illiquid. Bank investors should enter the NMTC Program with the understanding that the investment will most likely be held for the full seven-year compliance period; consequently, they should project taxable income for the duration of the investment term when determining their tax credit appetite. Bank investors should also consider that the NMTCs can be carried back one year and carried forward for 20 years.

Regulatory Issues

Accounting Issues

A bank can invest in NMTCs through direct investments into a bank-owned or third-party CDE (LP or LLC), or through a bank-owned Investment Fund (leverage structure transactions) or through a syndicated NMTC equity fund (LP or LLC). The accounting treatment for these investments is dictated by accounting rules governing partnerships and limited liability entities. Banks making investments in NMTC projects through direct investments or through leverage structure transactions should refer to the call report instructions (glossary sections Equity Method of Accounting and Subsidiaries) and generally accepted accounting principles for guidance on accounting for these investments.[55]

Investment Authority

National banks: Under the OCC's public welfare investment (PWI) authority, national banks may invest in NMTC and other community and economic development entities (CEDE) and projects that are designed primarily to promote the public welfare, as specified in 12 USC 24(Eleventh) and federal regulation 12 CFR 24. Regulation 12 CFR 24 states that a national bank or national bank subsidiary may invest directly or indirectly if the investment primarily benefits low- and moderate-income individuals, low- and moderate-income areas, or other areas targeted by a governmental entity for redevelopment, or the investment would receive consideration as a "qualified investment" under 12 CFR 25.23 of the CRA. Because NMTC investments generally meet these criteria, they are eligible under this authority.

Regulation 12 CFR 24 requires that a bank's aggregate PWIs and outstanding commitments, including the proposed investment, cannot exceed 15 percent of its capital and surplus. A bank needs written OCC permission, however, if its aggregate investments exceed 5 percent of capital and surplus. Furthermore, under 12 CFR 24, a bank's NMTCs and other PWIs may not expose it to unlimited liability.[56]

Regulation 12 CFR 24 requires banks to notify the OCC either through an after-the-fact notification or through a prior approval request process. Generally, a bank completes the CD-1-National Bank Community Development form to provide information about its PWI. The bank then sends the form to the Community Affairs Department of the OCC.[57]

If the CEDE[58] in which a national bank invests limits its activities to making loans to small businesses under the NMTC Program, the bank may invest in the CEDE either as an operating subsidiary or as a noncontrolling equity investment if the requirements in 12 CFR 5.34 or 5.36, respectively, are satisfied. Such investments are not subject to the limitations of 12 CFR 24.[59]

Federal savings associations: In addition to their general lending and investment authorities, federal savings associations (FSA) may use the following authorities to make PWIs, including investments in projects involving NMTCs:

- De minimis investments, under 12 CFR 160.36[60]
- Community development-related equity investments in real estate under
  - the Home Owners Loan Act (HOLA) 5(c)(3)(A)
  - 12 CFR 160.30
  - May 10, 1995 letter[61]
- Investments in Service Corporations and Lower-Tier Entities for community development investments, under 12 CFR 159[62]

Generally, an FSA is not required to seek approval for or provide notice to the OCC for public welfare investments using the de minimis authority (12 CFR 160.36) or the equity investments in real estate (HOLA 5(c)(3)(A)) that comply with the May 10, 1995 letter.[63] If the FSA meets the standards in the May 10, 1995 letter but is not eligible for expedited treatment pursuant to 12 CFR 116.5, then the FSA would be required to provide notice to the OCC Community Affairs Department at least 14 calendar days before making the investment. If the FSA does not meet the standards in the May 10, 1995 letter, then the FSA must seek a no-action letter from the OCC. Investments in service corporations and lower-tier entities for community development activities, under 12 CFR 159, are subject to prior notice to or approval by the OCC. The FSA should follow the filing requirements outlined under 12 CFR 159.11.

V. Who Is in the New Markets Tax Credit Program Today?

As of July 2012, 5,780 entities have been certified by the CDFI Fund as CDEs.[64] Through FY 2012, the most recent year of allocations, 749 award allocations have been made for a total of $36.5 billion. In the 2012 awards, more than half (58 percent) of the awardees (or sponsors) identified themselves as nonprofit organizations, followed by certified CDFIs (31 percent). Approximately 14 percent of awardees identified themselves as non-CDFI banks or bank holding companies. Nine percent identified themselves as real estate companies, and 15 percent as governmentally controlled entities.[65] Of the allocatees, 48 percent offer services nationally, 16 percent offer services across multiple states, 18 percent are limited to a single state, and 18 percent serve a local area. Based on the initial estimates of the allocatees, most (54 percent) of the investments are projected to be made in major urban areas,[66] with 24 percent projected in minor urban areas[67] and 22 percent in rural[68] areas.[69]

According to the NMTC Coalition, regulated financial institutions have been the principal source of investment capital for the program since its inception. In 2012, CDEs reported that 86 percent of QEI investment dollars secured in 2011 came from regulated depository institutions.[70]

In 2012, 82 percent of NMTC CDEs that responded reported using the leverage structure to raise capital. Leverage debt came from a variety of sources, including from an NMTC equity investor, a financial institution other than the equity investor, a charitable donor, the project sponsor, or another business entity. For most of these CDEs (89 percent), 100 percent of their investment capital used the leverage structure.[71]

VI. How Does the Cost and Pricing Structure Work?

An organization considering becoming an NMTC allocatee needs to consider how it will fulfill the requirements of a CDE, including

- outreach.
- fundraising.
- identifying and underwriting investment opportunities.
- loan processing.
- asset management.
- project outcome tracking and reporting.
- compliance with NMTC rules and regulations.

In addition, NMTC transactions such as QEIs or QLICIs require specialized legal and accounting skills. A single NMTC allocation is a seven-year commitment, and the competitive nature of the application process makes annual allocations uncertain. Allocatees need to consider sustainability strategies that will enable them to meet the asset management requirements over the compliance period, and the closing requirements as the transactions unwind after year seven.

Large-bank CDEs have developed specialized NMTC programs that are augmented by the bank's traditional commercial and institutional underwriters and credit committees. Typically, the large banks combine staff with investment and CDE responsibility. Smaller community banks, generally with assets greater than $1 billion, have also developed CDEs using a limited number of dedicated staff and drawing upon existing bank resources as needed. In at least one case, a consortium of community banks has used a CDE that is housed in a trade association.[72] Most CDEs draw on specialized consultants to help them set up compliance and project-tracking systems and to audit those systems on an ongoing basis.

The revenue to support CDEs comes from fees. A CDE can retain up to 15 percent of the QEIs it receives, although in practice the amount retained is usually less than 5 percent.[73] CDEs may also charge origination fees, management fees, and closing fees at the end of the compliance period. Fees are one consideration in NMTC applications, but competitive pressures tend to keep these fees well below market rates and allowable program maximums.

The revenue stream for investors comes from the tax credits and interest payments on their investments, and investors are generally experiencing market returns. In the standard transaction model, the return to the investor is based on how much of the tax credit subsidy is passed on to the borrower in the form of interest rate savings. In the leverage model, the return is based upon the relative contributions of the investor and the leverage lender. The price paid for the credits depends upon the time value of money and the market for credits. Based on the interviews that we conducted in 2011, investors were paying 65 to 73 cents on the dollar for credits, with most realizing returns in the range of 7.5 percent to 8.5 percent.

Leverage lenders receive interest-only payments on their loan over the course of the seven-year compliance period. Some leverage lenders, such as charitable or governmental entities, make leverage loans at significantly reduced interest rates. Bank leverage lenders typically realize returns at or near market rates.

VII. What Barriers Have Constrained the Growth of the NMTC Program?

Several factors have limited the growth of the NMTC Program:

Continuing congressional allocations: The NMTC Program requires continued allocations of credits from Congress. The Community Renewal Tax Relief Act of 2000 first authorized the NMTC Program through 2007. Subsequent legislation extended the program in one- or two-year increments, with the most recent authorization expiring in 2013.[74] The uncertainty of the program's future can be a disincentive for potential investors.

Limited credits: The amount of credits available to potential applicants is limited, making the award process very competitive. Over the first 10 years of the program, demand has outstripped the supply of tax credits by a margin of more than seven to one. The number of applicants for the 2011 round of allocation authority increased 26 percent over the number of applicants in 2010.

Costs and complexity: While continued innovation and development of the program has brought in new CDEs and leverage lenders, program complexity and high transaction costs can be significant barriers to new investors. NMTC regulations are complex, and penalties for noncompliance can be severe. Triggering recapture, even in the later years of the investment, can affect all of the credits previously claimed. The high, mostly fixed transaction costs have encouraged larger transactions, and limited the ability of smaller transactions to be economically feasible.

The CDFI Fund has been effective in promoting greater diversity among allocatees and investment types. The types of CDEs are quite diverse, and their numbers have increased every year. In addition, the IRS adopted rule changes that are designed to make it easier to invest in operating businesses.[75] These new rules are expected to help diversify the types of investments made through the program beyond real estate-related investments.

The introduction of the leverage structure has brought in new lenders, including public and philanthropic lenders who offer debt at below-market rates. These new leverage lenders have, in turn, encouraged investors into new geographic areas and different types of projects. Practitioners have remarked that there has been a significant surge in the number of new leverage lenders over the past few years.

The number and type of investors still tends to be very concentrated, however, with a large percentage of QEIs coming from banks, and a significant portion of that investment coming from a limited number of large financial institutions. These investors have traditionally had a strong appetite for NMTCs and a high degree of familiarity with the program's complex structures, making these investors an easy first choice for many CDEs.

The NMTC Program does not have many of the incentives for new investors that are in place for other types of credits, however. There also is little transparency around the performance of NMTC investments, so potential investors seldom have up-to-date information on market conditions, pricing, credit recapture, delinquencies, and yields on investments. There is no formal secondary market for NMTCs. And NMTCs do not have the flexibility of other credits in providing Alternative Minimum Tax relief or the option of using the effective-yield method of accounting.

CONCLUSION

The NMTC Program has been very successful in bringing new investment into low-income communities and channeling that investment into projects that provide quality jobs and services for residents of low-income communities, and that stimulate additional economic growth. Banks have been important partners in that process by establishing CDEs and receiving NMTC allocations, by investing in NMTC initiatives through their own CDEs and in other third-party CDEs, and by lending funds through leveraged transactions.

Participating in the NMTC Program helps banks meet customer needs by providing an additional tool for making commercial transactions in low-income communities that they might not otherwise be able to make. The subsidy provided through the NMTC Program can be flexibly applied to meet the needs of the borrower. The NMTC Program can help banks serve their communities, and NMTC investments may be eligible for positive CRA consideration. Finally, participation in the NMTC program can provide attractive financial returns to banks, including but not limited to the tax credits.

APPENDIX A: CASE STUDIES

Case Study One:
Standard Model Charter

School Facility
QLICI: $3 million

Project overview: A nonprofit acquires a vacant parochial school building in a low-income neighborhood, and is seeking financing to refurbish and update the classrooms and recreational facilities that will be leased to a charter school.

Tax credit project financing: A national bank-owned CDE uses its NMTC allocation to provide $3 million in financing to the QALICB, the nonprofit sponsoring the development of a charter school facility. The financing consists of a $3 million senior loan, developer cash equity of $50,000, and a municipal grant of $150,000 to purchase the existing building. The CDE, using the NMTC-enhanced standard financing structure, is the only private lender involved. The loan has a rate of 2.5 percent. Origination fees are half of what the bank normally charges its market rate customers. The loan is interest-only for seven years, a period that is substantially greater than the bank's normal practice. The LTV ratio is substantially higher than the bank's normal 70 percent ceiling. The loan will be refinanced after seven years without incurring any additional fees.

Case Study Two:
Standard Model
Business Loan Pool
QLICI: Ranges from $25,000 to $300,000

Project overview: A community bank with assets of $3 billion has a strong history of outreach that has provided a robust pipeline of loans to businesses throughout its service area. In some of the low-income areas, however, it has been difficult to make loans where property values and sales are weaker than normal. The areas are showing signs of some growth, largely from an active immigrant community, and before a recent recession the areas were seeing signs of an economic resurgence. The bank uses NMTCs to set up a loan pool that could provide low-interest loans with flexible terms to businesses located in these communities.

Tax credit project financing: A $20 million loan fund is created using NMTCs. The community bank provides two $10 million QEIs to capitalize the loan fund. The rates and terms of the loans available through the fund are standardized. Rates and fees are approximately half of market rates, and the term can range from one to five years. The loans fully amortize. The bank is able to remain in compliance with the "substantially all" test by relending the funds to additional borrowers as the principal is repaid on the initial loans made by the CDE. Loan officers originating commercial loans are required to check all business loans being rejected under conventional financing criteria for eligibility under this program.

Case Study Three:
Leverage Structure
Single-Bank Upgrade to an Existing Industrial Use
QLICI: $17 million

Project overview: A commercial lending department in a bank with a NMTC allocation has a loan request from an established customer looking to upgrade an existing facility where electric motors used in industrial applications are manufactured. The facility is located in a low-income neighborhood and has been a major employer in the area. The project is expected to create 100 well-paying jobs and retain 200 additional jobs by modernizing an aging industrial facility. The local industrial development authority has committed to provide $3 million in soft[76] debt. The completed facility has an appraised value of $25 million. The financials on the project are good, but the LTV is below bank credit standards.

Project financing: The commercial lending department contacts the community development department, and they determine that the project is eligible for NMTCs. An Investment Fund is created, with the community development department providing the equity portion of the investment ($4,773,600) and the commercial lending department providing the leverage loan ($12,226,400). Using the pooled funds, the Investment Fund makes a $17 million QEI into a bank-owned CDE. The CDE then makes two loans into the industrial business, a senior A-note at near market rates (6 percent) and a B-note at 1 percent interest, both with interest-only payments for seven years. (For the borrower, the blended interest rate is 4.6 percent.) The combined rate for the loans is approximately 300 basis points below market. The B-note has a put/call option that allows the business to purchase the note at a nominal rate at the end of the seven-year compliance period. Over the compliance period, the A- and B-notes earn $6,250,560 in interest, and the equity investment provides $6,630,000 in tax credits, providing a return to the bank of approximately 10.5 percent before taxes.

Case Study Four:
Leverage Structure
Pooled Third-Party Leverage Lender
Primary Health Care Facility
QLICI: $13 million

Project overview: A nonprofit agency is sponsoring the development of a new community health facility in an underserved low-income community. The new health facility will provide primary care to a community with very low rates of private health insurance coverage. Primary care in communities with low rates of private insurance has proven to lower public costs for emergency room care. The nonprofit agency has raised debt and grant contributions from a variety of sources, but a $3.5 million gap in the financing remains. The nonprofit agency pools all of this debt and grant funding, and offers this pooled funding as a leverage loan to a NMTC equity investor.

Project financing: The institutional lending department of the bank investor reviews the transaction and determines that the project will work with a NMTC investment. An Investment Fund is formed by the bank, a $3,650,400 bank equity investment is pooled with $9,360,000 from the nonprofit agency, and a $13 million QEI is made into the CDE. The CDE then lends the money into the project using an A-note and a B-note. The A-note earns near market rate interest, and the B-note, equivalent to the bank equity investment, earns 1 percent interest, with interest-only payments for the first seven years. A put/call option is put in place that allows the B-note to be purchased by the borrower at a nominal rate at the end of the compliance period. The bank equity investment earns $5,325,528 in interest and tax credits over seven years, providing a 6.5 percent return to the bank.

Case Study Five:
Leverage Structure
Multi-Bank Participation
Biomass Facility
QLICI: $80 million

Project overview: A company proposes a biomass facility that will create 150 new jobs in an area with high unemployment as a result of the collapse of the timber industry. The proposal is shown to a group of local bank representatives who then contact a CDE experienced in this type of development.

Project financing. Because the deal is bigger than any single bank can handle alone, the participation of multiple banks is necessary. The banks put together an $80 million QEI using the leverage structure. Two banks agree to provide $22,464,000 of equity into the transaction, and three banks provide $57,536,000 in debt financing as the leverage lender.

APPENDIX B: GLOSSARY OF TERMS

Allocatee: An applicant that receives an NMTC allocation.

Allocation agreement: Executed by the CDFI Fund and the allocatee, and the subsidiary allocatee, as applicable. The agreement contains terms and conditions governing the uses of the NMTC allocation, including, but not limited to, delineating service area(s) and targeted population(s) that the allocatee will serve and the favorable underwriting terms and conditions that will be used in providing financial assistance. The agreement also specifies events of default and recapture and the remedies available to the CDFI Fund, including reporting to the IRS, which would make the determination as to whether an event of recapture has occurred.

Areas of significant distress: Areas where the unemployment rate exceeds 1.5 times the national average, poverty rates exceed 30 percent , and median incomes are at or below 60 percent of area medians.

Community development entity (CDE): Any domestic corporation or partnership, for federal tax purposes, certified as a CDE by the CDFI Fund pursuant to IRC section 45D(c). Requirements for a CDE include that

- the primary mission of the entity is serving, or providing investment capital for, low-income communities or persons.
- the entity maintains accountability to residents of low-income communities through their representation on any governing board of the entity or on any advisory board to the entity.
- the entity is certified by the CDFI Fund as a CDE.

Gulf Opportunity (GO) Zone: That portion of the Hurricane Katrina disaster area determined to warrant assistance from the federal government to mitigate damage resulting from the hurricane. The Hurricane Katrina disaster area is an area that has been declared a major disaster area before September 14, 2005, under section 401 of the Gulf Opportunity Zone Act of 2005 (Public

L. 109-135), by reason of Hurricane Katrina. The GO Zone is in effect until December 31, 2014.

Low-income community (LIC):

Any population census tract where the poverty rate for such tract is at least 20 percent; or (1) in the case of a tract not located in a metropolitan area, the median family income for such tract does not exceed 80 percent of statewide median family income; or (2) in the case of a tract located within a metropolitan area, the median income for such a tract does not exceed 80 percent of the greater of statewide median family income or the metropolitan area median family income.

- Targeted areas that include the following:
  - High Out-Migration Rural County Census Tract: a population census tract within a county which, during the 20-year period ending with the year in which the most recent census was conducted, has a net out-migration of inhabitants from the county of at least 10 percent of the population of the county at the beginning of such period, if the median family income for the census tract does not exceed 85 percent of statewide median family income;
  - Low-Population/Empowerment Zone (EZ) Census Tract: a population census tract with a population of less than 2,000 if the tract is within an empowerment zone, and is contiguous to one or more low-income communities (not including other low-income communities in this category); and
  - Targeted population: certain individuals, or an identifiable group of individuals, including an Indian tribe, who (1) are low-income persons; or (2) otherwise lack adequate access to loans or equity investments.

NMTC allocation: An allocation of tax credit authority pursuant to the NMTC Program. A CDE that receives an NMTC allocation is an allocatee. If applicable, an allocatee may transfer all or part of its NMTC allocation to a subsidiary allocatee(s).

Qualified active low-income community business (QALICB): Any corporation (including a nonprofit corporation), partnership, or other business that meets the requirements set forth in IRC 45D(d)(2) and 26 CFR 1.45D-1(d)(4). Requirements for a QALICB include, but are not limited to, the following:

- At least 50 percent of the total gross income of such entity is derived from the active conduct of a qualified business within any low-income community.
- A substantial portion of the use of the tangible property of such entity (whether owned or leased) is within any low-income community.
- A substantial portion of the services performed for such entity by its employees are performed in any low-income community.

Qualified equity investment (QEI): An equity investment in a CDE that meets the requirements of IRC section 45D(b) and 26 CFR 1.45D-1(c). "Substantially all" of the investment must be made into a QLICI.

Qualified low-income community investment (QLICI): This term has the same meaning as set forth in IRC section 45D(d) and 26 CFR 1.45D-1(d). QLICIs include

- loans to, or capital or equity investments in, any QALICB.
- the purchase from a CDE of any loan made by such entity that is a QLICI.
- financial counseling and other services to businesses located in, and residents of, low-income communities.
- any equity investment in, or loan to, a CDE.

Standard transaction: The basic financing structure, in which the NMTC investor provides a QEI to a CDE, which, in turn, makes QLICIs to QALICBs.

Leverage structure transaction: A more complex financing structure, resulting from IRS Revenue Ruling 2003-20, that permits the QEI from an NMTC partnership entity, or Investment Fund, to include cash from a nonrecourse or recourse (pursuant to Revenue Ruling 2010-17) loan (debt) in addition to equity capital, thereby "leveraging" the NMTC investment.

Service area: The geographic area that encompasses the low-income communities in which the allocatee is authorized to make QLICIs using the proceeds of QEIs.

Standstill agreement: An agreement between a lender and a borrower in which the lender stops demanding the repayment of a loan. In the case of an NMTC leverage structure transaction, the borrower is the Investment Fund. Generally, the Investment Fund negotiates a standstill agreement to stop a leverage lender from foreclosing on a QALICB during the NMTC compliance period and threatening recapture of the tax credits.

"Substantially all" requirement: "Substantially all" of the equity investment in a CDE must be in QLICIs. Treasury Regulations section 1.45D-1(c)(5)(i) defines "substantially all" to mean at least 85 percent. The "substantially all" requirement must be satisfied for each annual period in the seven-year credit period. For the first annual period, the requirement is considered met if the calculation is performed on a single testing date and the result is at least 85 percent. For all subsequent annual periods, the "substantially all" requirement is considered met if the calculation is performed every six months and the average of the two computations for the annual period is at least 85 percent. In the seventh year of the seven-year credit period, 85 percent is reduced to 75 percent. See IRS LMSB-04-0510-016, *New Markets Tax Credit*, May 2010.

Targeted population:

As defined in 12 USC 4702(20) and related CDFI Fund and IRS guidance documents, "targeted population" refers to individuals, or an identifiable group of individuals, including an Indian tribe, who (1) are low-income persons; or (2) otherwise lack adequate access to loans or equity investments.

There are two categories of eligible targeted populations under the NMTC Program:

Low-income targeted population (LITP): The LITP is composed of low-income persons. An individual is considered to be "low-income" if the individual's family income, adjusted for family size, is not more than (1) for metropolitan areas, 80 percent of the area median family income; and (2) for nonmetropolitan areas, the greater of 80 percent of the area median family income, or 80 percent of the statewide nonmetropolitan area median family income.

GO Zone targeted population (GZTP): The GZTP is composed of individuals who were displaced from their principal residences and/or lost their principal source of employment as a result of Hurricane Katrina. In order to meet this definition, an individual's principal residence or principal source of employment, as applicable, must have been located in a population census tract within the GO Zone that contains one or more areas designated by the Federal Emergency Management Agency as flooded, having sustained extensive damage, or having sustained catastrophic damage as a result of Hurricane Katrina.

APPENDIX C

Resource Directory

Community Development Financial Institutions Fund
www.cdfifund.gov

CDFI Coalition
www.cdfi.org/cdfiinst.asp

New Markets Tax Credit Coalition
www.newmarketstaxcreditcoalition.org

Novogradac New Markets Tax Credit Resource Center
www.novoco.com/NMTC/index.shtml

OCC Fact Sheet on New Markets Tax Credits
www.occ.gov/cdd/Fact$_B$Sheet$_B$NMTC.pdf

OCC Public Welfare Investments (12 CFR 24) Resource Directory
www.occ.gov/topics/community-affairs/resource-directories/public-welfare-investments/ index-public-welfare-investments.html

End Notes

[1] U.S. Department of Housing and Urban Development, Public Law 106–554, appendix G, www.hud.gov/offices/cpd/ economicdevelopment/lawsandregs/laws/actof2000.pdf.

[2] The IRS has published regulations at 26 CFR 1.45D-1 and interpretative guidance to assist taxpayers claiming the tax credit(s) under Internal Revenue Code (IRC) section 45D.

[3] CDFI Fund, "New Markets Tax Credit Program," www_cdfifcmdgoviwhat_we do/programs_id.asp7programil:5_

[4] New Markets Tax Credit Coalition, The New Markets Tax Credit 10th Anniversary Report, December 2010 (www_nmtccoalition.org).

[5] CDFI Fund, Promoting Investment in Distressed Communities The New Markets Tax Credit Program, October 2008 Areas with signifirant levels of distress are defined in appendix B.

[6] An equity investment in a CDE. See appendix B for more information.

[7] U.S. Government Accountability Office, New Markets Tax Credit The Credit Helps Fund a Variety of Projects in Low Income Communities, But Could be Simplified, GA0-10-334, January 2010.

[8] Individual projects can vary significantly. In addition, fees and the method of financing affect how, and how much of, the subsidy reaches the borrower. According to our interviews of

industry professionals, fees and expenses can reduce the amount of the subsidy to 15 percent to 20 percent.

[9] New Markets Tax Credit Coalition, New Markets Tax Credit Progress Report 2012, June 2012.

[10] See definition of a low-income community in appendix B.

[11] See definition of a target population in appendix B.

[12] See definition of areas with significant distress in appendix B.

[13] GAO, New Markets Tax Credit Appears to Increase Investment in Low-Income Communities, But Opportunities Exist to Better Monitor Compliance, GAO-07-296, January 2007.

[14] OCC, Charter School Financing Opportunities, Spring 2011.

[15] OCC, Community Developments Investments, "Bank Financing of Healthy-Foods Initiatives," August 2012.

[16] According to The New Markets Tax Credit 10th Anniversary Report, nearly 90 percent of CDEs reported providing debt at below-market interest rates.

[17] OCC, Investing in Solar Energy Using the Public Welfare Authority, July 2011.

[18] In February 2012, the USDA published an administrative notice on using the NMTC Program with the Business and Industry Guaranteed Loan Program, the Rural Energy for America Program, and the Biorefinery Assistance Program. See www.rurdev.usda.gov/Support Documents/an4625.pdf.

[19] Federal Register, Vol. 75, No 47, pp. 11646, 11648, and 11652, "Interagency Questions and Answers Regarding Community Reinvestment."

[20] On March 18, 2013, the OCC, Board of Governors of the Federal Reserve System, and the Federal Deposit Insurance Corporation (FDIC) released a notice and request for comment regarding proposed updates to Interagency Questions and Answers Regarding Community Reinvestment, Federal Register, Vol. 78, No. 52, pp. 16765–16775. The proposed updates address several issues, including the treatment of community development activities outside an institution's assessment area and investment in nationwide funds that invest in community development.

[21] The leverage structure is described in the next section.

[22] This term has the same meaning as set forth in IRC section 45D(d) and 26 CFR 1.45D-1(d). See appendix B for QLICI definition.

[23] See Me 4511(0(4

[24] As defined in LAC 1044 (c)(3).

[25] As defined in section 103 of the Community Development Banking and Financial Institutions Act of 1994.

[26] See IRS LMSB-04-0510-016, New Markets Tax Credit, May 2010.

[27] CDFI Fund, "New Markets Tax Credit Program," www.cdfifund.gov/what_we_do/programs_id.asp?programID=S.

[28] Tax Credit Advisor, The Winner's Circle Treasury Announces 2011 New Markets Tax Credit Allocation Awards, April 2012.

[29] CDFI Fund, New Markets Tax Credit Quali¿ed Equity Investments Report, February 4, 2013.

[30] New Markets Tax Credit Coalition, The New Markets Tax Credit Progress Report 2012, June 2012. The report uses data from the CDFI Fund for this statistic.

[31] See definition in appendix B.

[32] Given the competitive nature of the application process, CDEs may voluntarily commit to investing a minimum of 95 percent or more of the QEIs in QLICIs.

[33] To date, the majority of NMTC investments have related to real estate projects. To encourage working capital and equipment loans to non-real estate businesses, new regulations were adopted that allow a CDE that makes a QLICI in a non-real estate business to invest certain

returns of capital from these investments in unrelated CDFIs that are CDEs. See New Markets Tax Credit Non-Real Estate Investments, Federal Register Vol. 77, No. 189, pp. 59544–59547, September 28, 2012.

[34] Treasury Regulations section 1.45D-1(d)(5).

[35] Tax Relief and Health Care Act of 2006, Public Law 109-432, div. A, title I, part 102(b), 120 stat. 2922 (2006).

[36] GAO, Community Development Financial Institutions and New Markets Tax Credit Programs in Metropolitan and Nonmetropolitan Areas, GAO-12-547R, April 2012.

[37] Rounded from /4286 percent

[38] No fees are reflected in this example.

[39] See definition in appendix B for more information on the "substantially all" requirement.

[40] IRS Revenue Ruling 2003-20. See www.cdfifund.gov/docs/2003_nmtc_irs_borrowed_funds_Qual_equity_ invstmnt.pdf.

[41] Banks may be both investor and leverage lender on a leverage structure transaction.

[42] The leverage structure allows equity investors flexibility in pricing their purchase of tax credits. The amount of tax credits that can be claimed is fixed, given the amount of the QEI. In the leverage structure, the equity investor typically receives the entire amount of credits available from the QEI (including the equity and the borrowed funds). Because the relative contribution by the equity investor into the QEI can vary in a leverage transaction, so too can the return that the equity investor receives from the credits. For example, an equity investor receives $3.9 million in tax credits with a $10 million QEI, regardless of whether the investor contributed $2 million or $2.8 million of equity. Pricing is subject to market forces.

[43] A put option is a contract that gives the holder of the contract the right to sell all or a portion of its interest in a security to a specified entity at a predetermined price. Conversely, a call option gives the holder the right to purchase all or a portion of an interest in a security from a specified entity at a predetermined price. In the case of the NMTC leveraged structure, CDEs generally structure transactions so that the tax credit investor may "put" its tax credit equity to the QALICB or the QALICB may "call" the tax credit equity from the investor for a predetermined price at the end of the seven-year period. See GAO, The New Markets Tax Credit The Credit Helps to Fund a Variety of Projects In Low-Income Neighborhoods, But Could be Simpli¿ed, GAO-10-334, January 2010.

[44] In some cases, the interest earned on the B-note pays for asset management and servicing fees_

[45] The A-note of $7.2 million has an interest rate of 8 percent, and the B-note of $2.8 million has an interest rate of 1 percent, generating $643,200 in interest payments annually.

[46] More than a dozen states have developed programs that work similarly to the federal NMTC program but offer a reduction of state tax liability. Most are designed to work in tandem with the federal program.

[47] Historic rehabilitation tax credits provide a reduction in federal taxes in exchange for investments in the rehabilitation of historic buildings.

[48] The renewable-energy investment tax credit program reduces federal income taxes by offering a 30 percent tax credit to owners or long-term lessees for qualified property that meets established performance and quality standards.

[49] The OCC report "U.S. Bank Invests in Solar Installations In Affordable Housing Communities" (July 2011) includes an illustration of a transaction that twinned NMTC and ITC. The report can be found in Investing in Solar Energy Using the Public Welfare Investment Authority at www.occ.gov/static/community-affairs/community-developments-investments/ solar11/cdesolar11Bindex.htm.

[50] See appendix B for more information.

[51] Treasury Regulations section 1.45D-1(e)(2)(iii). See IRS LMSB-04-0510-016, New Markets Tax Credits (May 2010) for more information, including how redemption is defined for different types of CDEs.

[52] CDFI Fund, New Markets Tax Credit Program CDE Certification Question and Answer, July 2005.

[53] To encourage working capital and equipment loans to non-real estate businesses, new regulations were adopted that allow a CDE that makes a QLICI in a non-real estate business to invest certain returns of capital from these investments in unrelated CDFIs that are CDEs. See New Markets Tax Credit Non-Real Estate Investments, Federal Register, Vol. 77, No. 89, pages 59544–59547 (September 28, 2012).

[54] See appendix B for the definition of an allocation agreement.

[55] See Financial Accounting Standards Board (FASB) Accounting Standards Codification (ASC) 323-30, Investments— Equity Method and Joint Ventures–Partnerships, Joint Ventures, and Limited Liability Entities (formerly, EITF Issue No. 03-16, "Accounting for Investments in Limited Liability Corporations").

[56] 12 CFR 24.4(b).

[57] Each national bank making a PWI under 12 CFR 24 shall maintain in its files information adequate to demonstrate that its investments meet the public welfare beneficiary standards and investment limit requirements.

[58] A CEDE is an entity that makes investments or conducts activities that primarily benefit low- and moderate-income individuals, low- and moderate-income areas, or other areas targeted by a governmental entity for redevelopment, or would receive consideration as "qualified investments" under 12 CFR 25.23. The following is a nonexclusive list of examples of the types of entities that may be CEDEs: (1) national bank community development corporation subsidiaries; (2) private or nonbank community development corporations; (3) CDFI Fund-certified Community Development Financial Institutions or Community Development Entities; (4) limited liability companies or limited partnerships; (5) community development loan funds or lending consortia; (6) community development real estate investment trusts; (7) business development companies; (8) community development closed-end mutual funds; (9) nondiversified closed-end investment companies; and (10) community development venture or equity capital funds.

[59] See "Legal Authority for Bank Investments in Subsidiary Community Development Entities and New Markets Tax Credits" at www.occ.gov/topics/community-affairs/resource-directories/ public-welfare-investments/common-part-24- questions.html.

[60] Under the de minimis authority, the FSA may invest, in the aggregate, less than or equal to the greater of 1 percent of capital or $250,000 in community development investments of the type permitted for a national bank under 12 CFR 24, including investments in NMTCs.

[61] Under HOLA 5(c)(3)(A), the FSA may make investments in real property and obligations secured by liens on real property located in areas "receiving concentrated development assistance by a local government under Title I of the Housing and Community Development Act of 1974." To be permissible for investment, the real estate (including NMTC projects) must be located within a geographic area or neighborhood that receives assistance or is covered by, for example, the U.S. Department of Housing and Urban Development's Community Development Block Grant program. Under 12 CFR 160.30, which covers the general lending and investment powers of FSAs, an FSA's aggregate community development loans and equity investments may not exceed 5 percent of its total assets, provided that its equity investments do not exceed 2 percent of total assets. The qualitative

standards for such loans and investments are explained in an opinion of the Office of Thrift Supervision (OTS) Chief Counsel, dated May 10, 1995. If the FSA meets all the standards, then it would not need to provide notice to the OCC.

[62] Under the authority of 12 CFR 159, the FSA may make investments in service corporations and lower-tier entities that engage in community development activities. A service corporation may engage in certain preapproved activities, including those that serve primarily community, inner-city, or community development purposes, including investments in NMTC projects. The FSA may invest up to 3 percent of its assets in service corporations, but any amount exceeding 2 percent must serve "primarily community, inner-city, or community development purposes."

[63] The FSA should maintain appropriate documentation to ensure that its community development investments conform to the statutory and regulatory requirements governing those investment authorities.

[64] According to the CDFI Fund, 5,780 organizations were certified as CDEs as of July 31, 2012.

[65] Applicants could identify themselves in more than one category.

[66] Counties in metropolitan areas with a population greater than or equal to 1 million.

[67] Counties in metropolitan areas with a population of less than 1 million.

[68] Nonmetropolitan counties

[69] CDFI Fund, 2012 New Markets Tax Credit Program Allocations, 2013.

[70] NMTC Coalition, The New Markets Tax Credit Progress Report 2012, June 2012.

[71] Ibid.

[72] See Community Bankers Association of Indiana. The National Community Investment Fund also has an NMTC fund for CDFI banks.

[73] NMTC Coalition, New Markets Tax Credit 10th Anniversary Report. The report found that 96 percent of reporting CDEs had committed to investing at least 95 percent of their QEIs.

[74] The Gulf Opportunity (GO) Zone Act of 2005 allocated an additional $1 billion of NMTCs for qualified areas affected by Hurricane Katrina for three years; the Tax Relief and Health Care Act of 2006 provided a one-year allocation in 2006; and the Tax Extenders and Alternative Minimum Tax Relief Act of 2008 provided $3.5 billion in tax credits in 2008. The American Recovery and Reinvestment Act of 2009 allocated $3 billion in tax credits to be split equally between 2008 and 2009. The Tax Relief, Unemployment Insurance Reauthorization, and Job Creation Act of 2010 provided an allocation limit of $3.5 billion in NMTCs both in 2010 and in 2011, and the act extended for two years, through 2016, the carryover period for unused NMTCs. The American Taxpayer Relief Act of 2012 allocated $3.5 billion each to 2012 and 2013.

[75] New Markets Tax Credit Non-Real Estate Investments, Federal Register, Vol. 77, No. 189, pp. 59544–59547, September 28, 2012.

[76] Soft debt is debt, usually from a public or philanthropic source, that is subordinate to other debt in the project and repayment is required only when there is sufficient cash flow.

In: The New Markets Tax Credit
Editor: Marlin Barrett
ISBN: 978-1-63463-644-5

Chapter 3

NEW MARKETS TAX CREDIT: BETTER CONTROLS AND DATA ARE NEEDED TO ENSURE EFFECTIVENESS*

United States Government Accountability Office

WHY GAO DID THIS STUDY

In recent years, private investors have claimed more than $1 billion in NMTCs annually. The credits are combined with private loans and other public funds to support investments in low- income communities. GAO was asked to review the financial structure of NMTCs.

This report assesses: (1) the complexity and transparency of NMTC financial structures and controls over the size of federal subsidies; (2) what is known about the types and amounts of fees and other costs of the financial structures; (3) what is known about the equity remaining in low-income community businesses after the 7-year credit period; and (4) what is known about NMTC project failure rates. GAO reviewed Treasury NMTC data and surveyed CDEs that allocated credits to 305 projects in 2010-2012.

---

* This is an edited, reformatted and augmented version of the United States Government Accountability Office publication, GAO-14-500, dated July 2014.

What GAO Recommends

Treasury should issue further guidance on how other government programs can be combined with NMTCs; ensure adequate controls to limit the risks of unnecessary duplication and above- market rates of return; and ensure that more complete and accurate data are collected on fees and costs, the equity remaining in the business after 7 years, and loan performance.

Treasury agreed with GAO's recommendations to improve data collection on equity remaining and loan performance. Treasury said that a recently formed working group, that includes representatives from the Community Development Financial Institutions Fund and the Internal Revenue Service, is considering GAO's other recommendations.

What GAO Found

The financial structures of New Markets Tax Credit (NMTC) investments have become more complex and less transparent over time. The increased complexity is due, in part, to combining the NMTC with other federal, state, and local government funds. Based on GAO's survey of Community Development Entities (CDEs) an estimated 62 percent of NMTC projects received other federal, state, or local government assistance from 2010 to 2012. While combining public financing from multiple sources can fund projects that otherwise would not be viable, it also raises questions about whether the subsidies are unnecessarily duplicative because they are receiving funds from multiple federal sources. In addition, in some cases the complexity of the structures may be masking rates of return for NMTC investors that are above market rates. For example, a study done for the Department of the Treasury (Treasury) found an investor apparently earning a 24 percent rate of return, which is significantly above market rates of return. In that case, the investor leveraged the NMTCs by using other public funds to increase the base for claiming the NMTC. Treasury and the Internal Revenue Service issued guidance about allowable financial structures in the early years of the NMTC program, but the guidance has not been updated to reflect the subsequent growth in complexity, such as the use of other public money to leverage the NMTC. Treasury also does not have controls to limit the risk of unnecessary duplication in government subsidies or above market rates of returns. Without such guidance and controls the impact of the NMTC program on low-income communities could be diluted. The costs of complex NMTC financial structures may not be fully reflected in fees charged by CDEs, and they could be reflected in other costs such as higher interest rates. Treasury has taken steps to ensure businesses are better informed about fees and other costs, but is not collecting these additional data itself. Without these data, Treasury is limited in its ability to analyze NMTC program benefits.

GAO also found that the data on equity remaining in businesses after the 7-year credit period were unreliable because, in part, instructions on what to report are unclear. As a result, at this time it is not possible to determine how much equity remains in low-income community businesses after 7 years.

Similarly, data on NMTC project failure rates were unavailable. GAO reviewed data of performance on loans from CDEs to low-income community businesses as an indicator of whether the businesses will be viable over the long term. However, data on loan performance were also incomplete because some reporting of this information by CDEs is optional. As a result, it is not possible to determine, at this time, the NMTC project failure rate with certainty.

Abbreviations

CDE	Community Development Entity
CDFI	Community Development Financial Institutions
CIIS	Community Investment Impact System
HTC	historic tax credit
IRS	Internal Revenue Service
LIC	low-income community
LIHTC	Low-Income Housing Tax Credit
NMTC	New Markets Tax Credit
QEI	qualified equity investment

* * *

July 10, 2014

The Honorable Tom Coburn, M.D.
Ranking Member
Committee on Homeland Security and Governmental Affairs
United States Senate

Dear Dr. Coburn:

Congress established the New Markets Tax Credit (NMTC) program as part of the Community Renewal Tax Relief Act of 2000 to encourage investors to invest in impoverished, low-income communities that traditionally lack access to capital.[1] Conventional access to credit and investment capital for developing small businesses, creating and retaining jobs, and revitalizing neighborhoods is often limited in economically distressed communities or in communities with large low-income populations. The NMTC provides investors (individuals, financial institutions, other corporations, etc.) with a tax credit for investing in communities that are economically distressed or consist of low-income populations. The investors are able to claim a credit equal to 39 percent of eligible investment spread over 7 years.

The NMTC program is administered by the Community Development Financial Institutions (CDFI) Fund in the Department of the Treasury (Treasury) which allocates tax credit authority—the amount of investment which investors use as the base for determining the amount of tax credits they are eligible to claim—to Community Development Entities (CDE) that apply for and obtain allocations. These CDEs in turn offer the tax credits to private investors in exchange for equity investments with the CDEs. The CDEs then invest the capital they raise in qualified low-income community businesses. The resulting NMTC financial structures include the CDEs, investors, and qualified low-income community businesses— as well as the transactions between them—and may also include private loans and funding from other government programs.

We have issued three reports on the status and initial results of the NMTC program.[2] You asked us to follow up on these reports and review the NMTC financial structures and the amount of equity investment flowing through to qualified low-income community businesses. Our objectives were to assess: (1) NMTC financial structures in terms of their complexity, transparency, and their effect on the size of the federal subsidies going to NMTC projects, as well as controls to ensure that subsidies are not larger than necessary for the investment; (2) what is known about the types and amounts of fees and other costs that reduce the amount of equity reaching low-income community businesses; (3) what is known about the amount of equity left in the low-income community businesses after the 7-year credit period; and (4) what is known about the NMTC projects that are at risk of failing by becoming economically nonviable.

Our assessment criteria for objective 1 were drawn from our prior work evaluating tax expenditures, which discuss complexity (or simplicity), transparency, and duplication, as well as from internal control standards about the efficient use of resources.[3] For objective 1, we reviewed the NMTC literature and interviewed representatives of CDEs and researchers who have evaluated the program to determine how the financial structures have evolved, and conducted and analyzed the results of a survey of CDEs to determine how the NMTC has been combined with other federal tax benefits, grants, and other assistance.[4] Our criteria for objectives 2, 3, and 4 were GAO criteria for valid data— that they be sufficiently accurate and complete to capture program performance. For objective 2, we analyzed data from the CDFI Fund on fees (actual and projected) that CDEs charged to projects with loans and investments originating in 2011 and 2012. (The CDFI Fund started collecting these additional data on fees in 2011 based on our recommendation.[5]) For objective 3, we analyzed data from the CDFI Fund on the projected equity remaining in the business for projects beginning in 2011-2012. The CDFI Fund requires CDEs to project equity remaining in businesses for loans and investments originating in 2011 or later. For objective 4, we analyzed data reported by CDEs to the CDFI Fund that could indicate that a project is experiencing financial distress, such as whether a loan on a project is delinquent, charged off, or restructured.

We conducted this performance audit from May 2013 to July 2014 in accordance with generally accepted government auditing standards. Those standards require that we plan and perform the audit to obtain sufficient, appropriate evidence to provide a reasonable basis for our findings and conclusions based on our audit objectives. We believe that the evidence obtained provides a reasonable basis for our findings and conclusions based on our audit objectives. See appendix I for more details about our scope and methodology.

BACKGROUND

The CDFI Fund is authorized to allocate tax credit authority to CDEs that manage NMTC investments in low-income community development projects. The CDEs are domestic corporations or partnerships with a primary mission of providing investment capital for low-income communities or low-income persons. Some CDEs are established by other public or private entities, such as local governments or financial institutions. Through the CDFI Fund, Treasury awards tax credit authority to CDEs through a competitive application process. After CDEs are awarded tax credit authority, they use it to attract investments from investors who then claim the NMTC. CDEs use the money raised to make investments in projects (one or more) in low-income communities. In the 11 rounds of allocations since 2003, Treasury, through the CDFI Fund, has made allocations to CDEs that total $40 billion.

The base for claiming the credit on a project is called the qualified equity investment (QEI). It equals the credit authority allocated to a project by a CDE and generally covers a portion of the total project costs. The equity in the QEI includes money provided by NMTC investors but may also include money from private lenders or other government entities. The NMTC, which is equal to 39 percent of the QEI, is claimed over 7 years—5 percent in each of the first 3 years and 6 percent over each of the last 4 years. In recent years, private investors have claimed more than $1 billion in NMTCs annually. When the QEI does not cover the entire project cost, the NMTC financing is supplemented by other financing outside the NMTC allocation.

CDEs are required to invest the funds they receive in qualified low-income community investments, which include, but are not limited to, investments in operating businesses and residential, commercial, and industrial projects. Although the range of activities financed by CDEs varies, about half of NMTC investments have been used for commercial real estate projects. The program expired in 2013 but legislation has been proposed to extend it, and the President requested a permanent extension in his fiscal year 2015 budget proposal.[6]

The Financial Structures of NMTC Investments Have Become More Complex and Less Transparent While Treasury Guidance Covers Only the Simpler Structures

NMTC investors have developed financial structures that increase the amount of other funding from either private or public sources that are used with the NMTC—a process that is called increasing the leverage on the investment. These structures can increase the amount of federal subsidy to a project and can result in projects being undertaken that would not otherwise have been started for lack of sufficient funding. However, they also increase the complexity of the financial structures by adding more parties and more transactions, which in turn reduces transparency and may increase the cost in terms of fees and other related transactions costs. An assessment of the NMTC program as a whole requires complete information on all the costs and benefits attributable to the NMTC, including these administrative and compliance costs.[7]

Figures 1-4 are simplified illustrations of these increasingly complex financial structures.[8]

In 2003, the Internal Revenue Service (IRS) confirmed the ability to use private funding to leverage a NMTC structure.[9] Also, in 2004, Treasury issued final regulations generally allowing the NMTC to be combined with other tax credits.[10] However, neither Treasury nor IRS has specifically confirmed the ability to use other federal or state funding to increase the leverage on NMTC investments.

In Practice, NMTC Financial Structures Are More Complex

Many NMTC projects have financial structures that are more complex than the simple examples in figures 1 through 4. According to CDFI Fund data, 21 percent of projects originating in 2010 through 2012 had financial structures involving more than one CDE. In addition, 21 percent of projects had four or more transactions involving financial flows (such as loans from the CDEs to the LIC business). The NMTC financial structures have become more complex over time. We estimated that 41 percent of NMTC investments were made using one of the leveraged models in 2006, while more recent industry estimates state that more than 90 percent used such leverage in 2013.[11]

The simplified structures in our examples also do not show some of the complexities that are required for the purpose of acquiring the tax benefit. For example, when the public funds are leveraged, as in figure 4, a pass- through entity that is disregarded for tax purposes is established to route the flow of funds back from the low-income community business to the investment fund to claim the NMTC. The complexity of the structures may reduce transparency by making it more difficult to trace the flow of private and public funds and the benefits from the tax subsidies. For example, investors can leverage other tax credits with the NMTCs to gain access to other tax benefits such as when the tax credit for solar equipment is leveraged to claim additional NMTCs and also claim accelerated depreciation deductions based on the solar equipment.

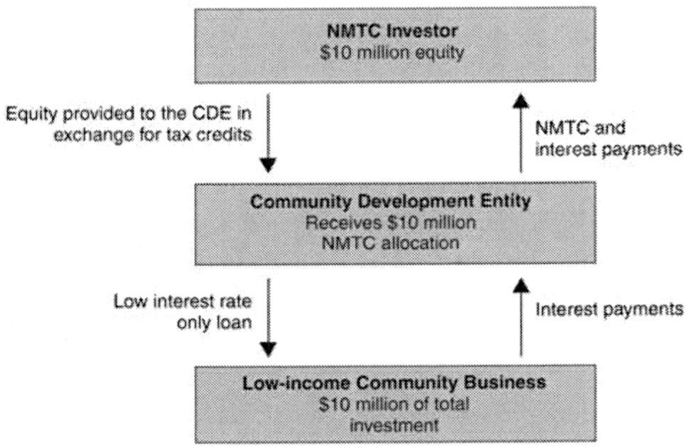

In the most basic of the NMTC financing structures, an investor contributes funds directly to a community development entity (CDE). The CDE has received authority from the CDFI Fund to issue tax credits for a $10 million project. The investor invests $10 million for 7 years and receives a tax credit of 39 percent on the $10 million. At the end of the 7 years, all or a portion of the investor's equity is returned, and the low-income community (LIC) business may now be in a position to obtain more conventional financing.

The return the investor earns is a combination of the tax credits plus interest payments made by the LIC business. The investor incurs some project related risks since the LIC business interest payments are not necessarily guaranteed and the business could go bankrupt and fail to repay the loan made by the CDE.

The investor earns an annual rate of return of approximately 6 percent based on the credits alone which are claimed over the 7-year compliance period.[a]

For the investor to receive a return equal to the market rate of return – which for this and the following example is assumed to be 7 percent – the CDE could charge an interest rate to the LIC business as low as 1 percent.

Revenue Effects: The present value of the lost tax revenue to the federal government is $3.46 million – the present value of the $3.9 million in tax credits paid over 7 years evaluated at the federal government's 7-year borrowing rate of about 3 percent.

Source: GAO analysis. |GAO-14-500.

[a] This rate of return represents the internal rate of return of the $10 million investment in terms of the value of the tax credits. The tax credit is 5 percent of the investment amount in each of the first 3 years and 6 percent in each of the last 4 years during the 7-year compliance period.

Figure 1. Simplified Example of a New Markets Tax Credit (NMTC) Basic Model.

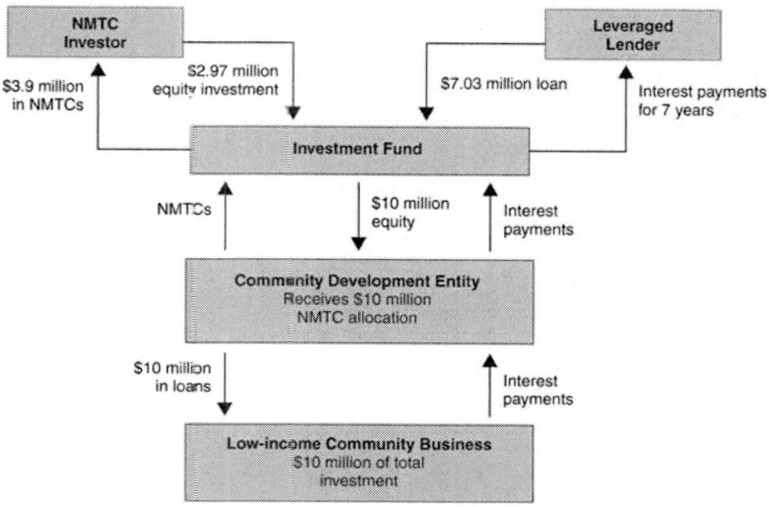

In this model the equity is combined in an investment fund with a loan from a leveraged lender. The NMTC investor receives tax credits on the full amount of the equity plus the loan. The equity investment is generally not paid back to the investor at the end of the compliance period. The leverage lender receives interest payments throughout the 7-year compliance period and unless refinanced, the loan amount is repaid at the end of the compliance period.

The borrowed funds and the equity investor's cash are used by the CDE to make an investment (usually in the form of loans) to the LIC business. The CDE then passes the tax credits and interest earned on the investment (less any fees) back to the investment fund, where they are distributed to the equity investor and leverage lender.

In the example, the allocation is again $10 million but in this case the investor puts $2.97 million into the fund and the leveraged lender loans the remaining $7.03 million. The investor's $2.97 million is the present value to the investor of the stream of tax credits that will be generated by the investment evaluated at the 7 percent rate of return. The investor incurs limited project related risk since the credit can be claimed whether the low-income community business succeeds or not.[a]

Effect on Complexity: The complexity of this structure creates added cost from the resources used to create entities like the investment fund and to negotiate the terms of the investment among an increasing number of participants.

Revenue Effects: The present value of the tax revenue loss to the government is $3.46 million as in figure 1.

Source: GAO analysis. | GAO-14-500.

[a] The investor's risk is largely limited to "recapture" risk where the IRS reclaims credits from prior years as well as future credits due to issues related to CDE compliance with IRS regulatory requirements. See GAO, *New Markets Tax Credit: The Credit Helps Fund a Variety of Projects in Low-Income Communities, but Could Be Simplified,* GAO-10-334 (Washington, D.C.: Jan. 29, 2010) for a description of the events that can trigger a "recapture" of the credit.

Figure 2. Simplified Example of New Markets Tax Credit (NMTC) Investment Leveraged with Private Funds.

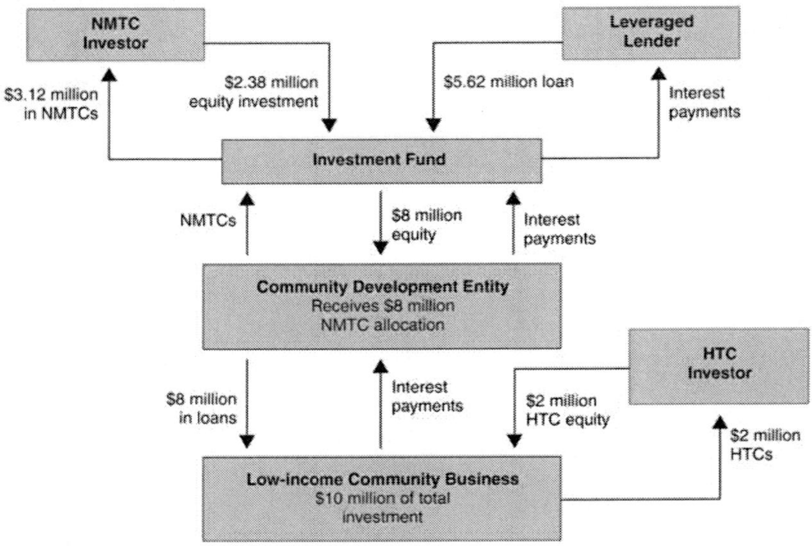

The leveraged structure can also be used with other public subsidies such as grants and tax credits where the subsidies are not part of the leverage structure; i.e., the grant or tax credit is not combined with the NMTC equity in the investment fund to serve as the basis for NMTCs. In contrast to figure 2, the CDE has only an $8 million NMTC allocation for the $10 million project but, in this example, all $10 million of the project's expenditures also qualify for a federal tax credit for rehabilitating historic structures. The historic tax credit (HTC) rate is 20 percent which yields an HTC of $2 million.

The NMTC that can be claimed on the $8 million allocation is $3.12 million which has a present value to the investor of $2.38 million (evaluated at the 7 percent rate of return) which the investor puts into the investment fund. The remainder of the $8 million required to claim the NMTC is provided by the leveraged loan of $5.62 million. The additional $2 million required to fund the $10 million project is provided directly to the LIC business as equity by the HTC investor.

Effect on Complexity: The complexity in this case arises, in part, from the need to create additional financial entities for different types of public funds. For example, the HTC investor uses a master tenant partnership (not shown in figure 3) to receive the HTCs and make the HTC equity investment in the LIC business.

Revenue Effects: In this case, the revenue cost sums to $4.76 million – $2.76 million (the present value of the $3.12 million of NMTCs) plus the $2 million of HTCs.

Source: GAO analysis. |GAO-14-500.

Figure 3. Simplified Example of a New Markets Tax Credit (NMTC) Investment Combined with (but Not Leveraged by) Other Public Funds.

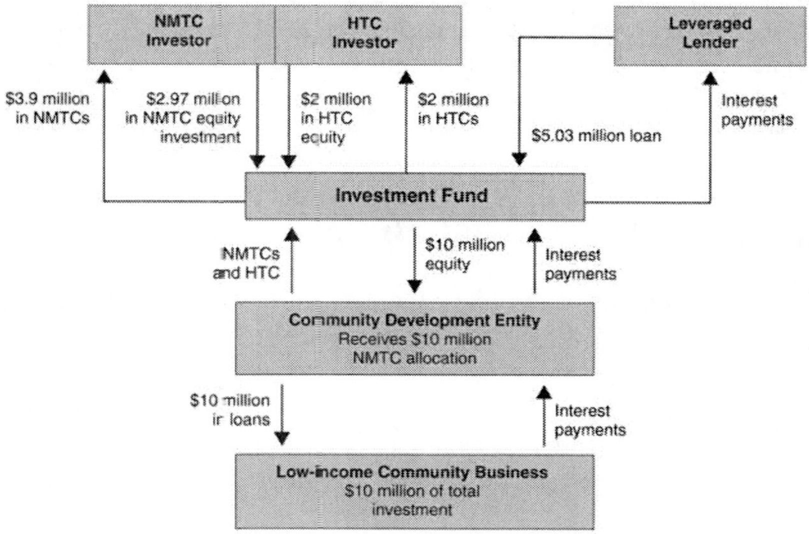

Other government subsidies can also be part of the leveraged structure; i.e., the grant or tax credit can be combined with the NMTC equity in the investment fund to serve as the basis for NMTCs. In figure 4, the investor claims the NMTC on the value of HTCs as well as on the NMTC equity and leveraged loan. The NMTC investor community often refers to this practice as "twinning" the NMTC with other tax credits or public assistance.

The project has a $10 million NMTC allocation (rather than the $8 million in figure 3) and, as before, $10 million of expenditures that qualify for the HTC yielding a $2 million HTC.

The NMTC investor provides $2.97 million in equity but in this case the leveraged lender provides $5.03 million for a total of $8 million. By including the $2 million HTC, the investment fund is brought up to $10 million. Unlike figure 3, the NMTC investor claims the credit on the full $10 million.

Effect on Complexity: As in the previous example, complexity arises from the need to create additional financial entities for different types of public funds. But in this case, because the funds are pooled, additional effort is required to ensure that the funds are properly spent. For example, the HTC equity that qualifies for the NMTC in the investment fund must be used for the qualified rehabilitation expenditures that form the basis of the HTC.

Revenue Effects: The present value of the $3.9 million in NMTCs is $3.46 million. The total foregone revenue to the government, including the HTC, is $5.46 million. The revenue cost is higher than in figure 3 because the HTC was used to leverage the NMTC.

Source: GAO analysis. |GAO-14-500.

Figure 4. Simplified Example of New Markets Tax Credit (NMTC) Investment Leveraged with Both Private and Public Funds.

However, as mentioned above, this complexity can have benefits because it may result in projects getting financing they could not get otherwise. For example, combining assistance from other government programs with the NMTC, as in figures 3 and 4, could finance projects that would not be viable if they had to rely on only the NMTC and private lenders for financing as in figure 2.

A Majority of NMTC Projects Used Other Public Funds in 2010-2012

Based on our survey of CDEs with projects originating in 2010-2012, the use of other public sources of funds with the NMTC is widespread (as shown in Table 1). An estimated

- Sixty-two percent of all NMTC projects received other public funding—funds from federal, state or local public sources;
- Thirty-three percent of all NMTC projects received other federal funding; and
- Twenty-one percent of all NMTC projects received funding from multiple other government programs.

Among the most frequently used other federal sources by NMTC projects in our survey were historic tax credits (HTC) and tax-exempt bonds for private non-profit education facilities. In addition, for a number of NMTC projects in our survey, small business participants obtained loans guaranteed by the Small Business Administration. The other federal funds most often leveraged with the NMTC projects in our survey were the historic tax credits, Recovery Zone bonds and tax-exempt bonds for private non-profit education facilities. The state and local funds most frequently leveraged with the federal NMTC were state historic tax credits and state new markets tax credits[12] (see appendix II for additional results from our survey).

The use of multiple other government programs raises questions about unnecessary duplication. The CDFI Fund currently asks CDEs whether other public funds are used to finance projects but does not ask for any details such as the information on specific programs providing those funds. Therefore, it is not possible at this time to determine whether unnecessary duplication is occurring because of a lack of data.

Complex NMTC Financial Structures May Mask Investments with Rates of Return That Are Higher Than Necessary

The competitive or market return should be sufficient to attract enough investors to fund the project because it reflects the return on comparable investments with similar risk. In figures 1 through 4 above, we assumed for illustrative purposes that the competitive market rate of return was 7 percent. We also assumed that NMTC investors provided enough equity to the project (perhaps because of competition for the credits) that the credits claimed over the 7-year compliance period provided a market return.

NMTC industry representatives have argued that competition for credits by potential investors and competition between CDEs for credit allocations works to ensure returns on NMTC investments are kept at market rates commensurate with NMTC investor's risk. The NMTC investor's level of risk depends on the financial structure that the investor uses. For example, when the NMTC investor uses a leveraged investment model, the investor does not generally share in the riskiness of the project. Unless the investor is also the leveraged lender or has some other financial interest in the project, it is not exposed to any risk from project failure because such an event generally does not stop the investor from claiming the credit.

Some evidence suggests that some investors may receive returns that are above-market and therefore more than the necessary subsidy required to attract the funds. In a case study reported by the Urban Institute, an investor appeared to put in about $500,000 of NMTC equity to claim $1.2 million of NMTCs representing a return of about 24 percent compounded annually.[13] The NMTC was leveraged entirely with $2.5 million of federal and state HTCs without use of a conventional leveraged loan in the NMTC structure. As a result, 83 percent of the qualified equity investment on which an investor claimed NMTCs was provided by other federal and state tax credit programs.

However, the Urban Institute study authors said that, because of the complex financial structure, they could not rule out the possibility that the investor supplied other, non-NMTC funds to the project and at a lower rate of return. They noted that the NMTC financing was combined with a conventional loan outside the NMTC structure, owner equity, and a loan from the local municipality. If the NMTC investor supplied some of these additional funds, it is possible that the investor's overall rate of return may have been lower and more in-line with the market return.

Table 1. Estimated Percentage of Projects Receiving Other Federal Funding (Projects Originating in 2010-2012)

Type of Federal Funding	Percent of All NMTC projects	95 percent confidence interval[a]	Funding amount ($ millions)	95 percent confidence interval ($ millions)
Tax credits	8	5-12	353	59-647
Tax-exempt bonds	6	4-11	2,023	874–3,172
Grants	11	7-17	449	258-639
Loans	11	7-16	740	271-1,209
Total	**33**	**27-39**	**3,565**	**2,317-4,813**

Source: GAO survey of NMTC projects originating in 2010-2012. | GAO-14-500

Note: Total percent of projects receiving other federal funding does not equal sum of components because some projects used more than one type of federal funding.

[a] A 95 percent confidence interval means that if you were to determine an estimate for different probability samples, 95 out of 100 times the confidence interval would include the actual population value. In other words, the actual population value is between the lower and upper limits of the confidence interval 95 percent of the time.

Guidance and Controls Do Not Exist to Prevent above-Market Rates of Return or Unnecessary Duplication and Costs

Internal controls should provide reasonable assurance that operations and use of resources are efficient. In the context of the NMTC program, the resources administered by Treasury include the tax benefits claimed by the NMTC investors. One NMTC control has been Treasury and IRS guidance on allowable financial structures. The Secretary of the Treasury has the authority to limit how other federal tax benefits are used with the NMTC and the Secretary has used this authority to prohibit its use with the Low-Income Housing Tax Credit (LIHTC).[14] While an IRS revenue ruling, issued in 2003, allowed using debt to leverage NMTC equity, the ruling did not explicitly address using other public funds, such as other tax benefits, to leverage the NMTC as in figure 4.

Controls do not exist to monitor and prevent unnecessary use of other public funds to supplement the NMTC. As already noted, Treasury, through the CDFI Fund, does not collect information about the specifics of other public funding. For the CDFI Fund, Treasury does not have controls to limit the risk of cases like the example from the Urban Institute study where other public funds were used to expand the NMTC base and apparently generate a 24 percent rate of return for the NMTC investor.

We believe that such controls could take a variety of forms and would have to be assessed relative to any added compliance and administrative costs. A control that would provide greater clarity about tax subsidies could be achieved by requiring CDEs to report the NMTC investor's overall rate of return on the NMTC project. As suggested by the Urban Institute example, this information would allow an assessment of whether the NMTC investor is earning a market return commensurate with the risk on its entire investment. With this information, an additional control could be implemented that would require CDEs to justify rates of return above a certain threshold by explaining why this project was so risky that it required a greater-than-market rate of return. Other controls that could be considered include caps on rate of returns and mechanisms to ensure competition among NMTC investors sufficient to prevent above-market rates of return. The decision to adopt any of these controls would require that Treasury compare the benefits of the controls with any compliance costs from added complexity for taxpayers and administrative costs for Treasury from collection and evaluation of the data and monitoring the controls once they are put in place.

The complexity of the financial structures creates a lack of transparency for taxpayers and IRS, and can increase both the risk of higher than needed NMTC rates of return and investment transactions costs. Combining multiple investment sources may help some NMTC projects to obtain sufficient financing to proceed. Indeed, NMTCs are often referred to as "gap financing" that can be added to other financing. Some projects may not require NMTC funding. The Urban Institute study estimated that about 20 percent of projects in the first 4 years of the program showed no evidence of needing NMTCs to proceed while about 30-40 percent did with 30 percent uncertain.

However, even in the case where the NMTC funding is necessary, the intricate patterns of investment flows through NMTC structures, where multiple sources may be mingled and later dispersed, make it difficult to determine who is receiving subsidies and whether the return to NMTC investors is higher than necessary. In addition, the network of transactions in the NMTC financial structures increase costs both in terms of explicit CDE fees and other resources used to pay the legal and accounting costs necessary to establish the entities that make the transactions.[15]

Fees and Retentions Reduce the Available NMTC Equity but Lack of Transparency Makes the Size of the Reduction Uncertain

Fees and retentions directly reduce the amount of tax subsidized equity investment that is available to low-income community businesses but these costs do not represent the only way that equity can be reduced. The costs associated with financial structures could also appear in the form of higher interest rates, especially when the investor and leveraged lenders are related parties. In listening sessions organized by CDFI Fund officials, some CDEs reported that comparison of the fees that they charged to the fees charged by integrated investors/lenders were inaccurate because of the ability of integrated investors/lenders to receive compensation in other ways.

The fees, interest, and other costs that can offset one another (a low fee may be offset by a high interest rate) also reduce transparency by making the net effect on the tax subsidized equity reaching the low-income community business hard to determine. Officials at the CDFI Fund are attempting to address this issue by requiring CDEs to provide a disclosure statement to low-income community businesses about the size of tax subsidized equity and how it is affected by fees and interest rates.[16] The new requirement that CDEs disclose to the low-income community businesses all transactions costs, fees, and compensation could help those businesses understand the final net benefit to the project being financed with NMTCs. However, because Treasury does not require the CDFI Fund to collect the CDE disclosure statements itself, the CDFI Fund database has incomplete information about fees, interest, and other costs. Without such complete information the Treasury is limited in its ability to analyze the final net financial benefit of NMTC investments to low-income community businesses.

CDE Fees and Retentions Reduce the NMTC Equity Available to the Low- Income Community Businesses

Our analysis shows that fees and retentions by the CDEs reduced the $8.8 billion of NMTC investment available to the businesses in 2011-2012 by about $619 million or 7.1 percent. The initial reduction occurred as part of the NMTC investment that the CDEs retain to cover administrative costs before investing the remainder in the project.

The CDEs then also charge fees over the course of the 7-year compliance period that further reduces the equity available to the project. These fees can take the form of front-end or origination fees at closing, on-going, or asset management fees during the compliance period, and closing fees at the end of the compliance period.

Table 2 shows the fees and retentions measured as a percentage of NMTC investment that reduce the equity that is available to the businesses. In addition, the projects may also incur third-party transaction costs for NMTC related accounting or legal services not provided by the CDEs. The CDEs are not required to report these other third-party transaction costs to the CDFI Fund.

Higher CDE Fees and Retentions Are Associated with More Complex Financial Structures

Our analysis also shows that the amount of fees and retentions charged is strongly associated with the amount of NMTC investment in the project: the amount of NMTC investment accounts for about 50 percent of the variation in fees across projects.

Although the CDFI Fund does not currently collect data that directly measure the complexity of investment structures, it does collect data on the number of investment transactions that occur on a NMTC project. These transactions often represent loans and investments to the business from different entities such as multiple CDEs, and can therefore be used as a proxy for more direct measures of complexity. Our regression analysis of these data shows that higher fees and retentions are associated with more complex structures as indicated by the number of transactions (see table 3 for details of this association between fees and retentions and financial structure, and other characteristics of the NMTC project).

Fees and retentions are generally described by NMTC participants as reflecting mostly fixed costs, which would be more consistent with fees decreasing in proportion to the total size of the NMTC investment.

Table 2. New Markets Tax Credit (NMTC) Investment Retained and Fees Charged by Community Development Entities (CDEs), 2011-2012

Fee Types	Average fees ($ millions)	Total fees for all projects ($ millions)	Total fees as a percent of total NMTC investment[a]
NMTC investment retained by CDEs	0.2	170	1.9
CDE professional fees charged			
at or prior to close (front-end)	0.2	183	2.1
during compliance period (on-going)	0.2	198	2.3
at or after investment exit (back-end)	0.1	67	0.8
Subtotal	0.6	448	5.1
Total	**0.8**	**619**	**7.1**

Source: GAO analysis of CDFI Fund data. | GAO-14-500

Notes: Components may not sum to totals due to rounding. Dollar amounts are not adjusted for inflation. The fees contain both actual and projected amounts. The earlier in the project's history the fees are paid, the more likely the payments are to be actual rather than planned. The totals and subtotals include $2,000 in average fees and $1.4 million in total fees in a fourth category of CDE professional fees called "other" fees by the CDFI Fund not listed separately in this table.

[a] The total qualified equity investment (QEI) for all projects originating in 2011-2012.

Table 3. Project Characteristics Associated with Fees and Retentions Charged by Community Development Entities (CDEs), 2011-2012

Project characteristics	Effect on fees and retentions	Size of the effect: Change in dollar value of fees and retentions
Amount of NMTC qualified equity investment	Increased	$7,800 per $100,000 of additional NMTC-qualified equity investment
Number of transactions as a proxy for financial structure complexity	Increased	$4,800 per additional transaction
Average interest rate	Increased	$9,600 per 1.0 percentage point increase in the interest rate on NMTC-related loans to the project

Project characteristics	Effect on fees and retentions	Size of the effect: Change in dollar value of fees and retentions
Purpose: business	Increased	$29,000 more in fees and retentions charged on transactions for business purposes than those for rehabilitation, or other purposes
Amount of non-public funds used on project	Decreased	$90 less in fees and retentions per $100,000 of private funds invested in the project
Poverty rate greater than 30 percent indicating distressed low-income community	Decreased	$3,000 less in fees and retentions for projects in communities with poverty rates exceeding 30 percent

Source: GAO analysis of CDFI Fund data. | GAO-14-500

Legend: NMTC = New Markets Tax Credit.

Notes: The table summarized results for selected variables of a regression analysis of the relationship of total fees and retentions with other project characteristics.

CDEs That Reported They Charged No Fees or Retentions Illustrates the Program's Lack of Transparency

For about 20 percent of projects originating in 2011-2012, CDEs reported to the CDFI Fund that they charged zero fees or retentions on these projects (see figure 5). However, it seems unlikely that the services provided by the CDEs were uncompensated. While the payment may have come in different forms, a lack of transparency makes it hard to readily determine how much of the NMTC investment is being reduced and by what means. For example, NMTC program participants have suggested that these projects with no fee costs may be more integrated investments where banks or other large institutions may be lenders as well as investors. In this case, low fees may be offset by higher interest rates. We found some indirect evidence of this in another regression where the projects with no fees or retentions were analyzed relative to all the projects that had fees and retentions. Here, the analysis showed that the projects with higher average interest rates were more likely to charge no fees and retentions. For this subgroup of projects, the positive relationship between fees and interest rates that we found when we analyzed all the projects (as shown in table 3) is reversed.

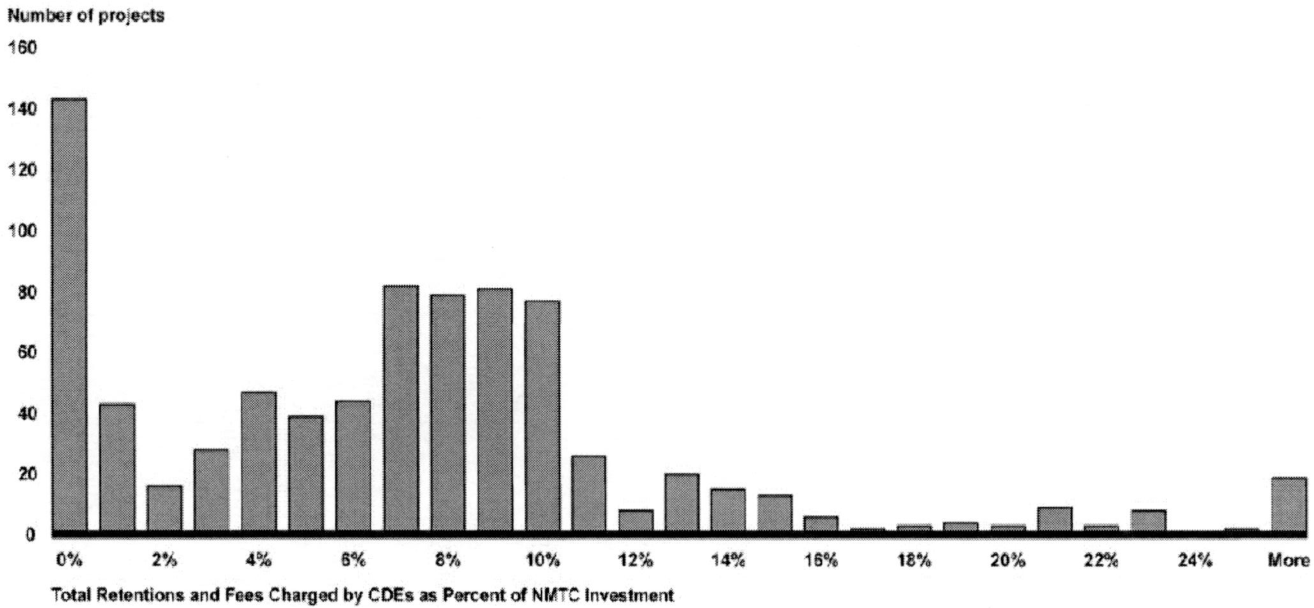

Source: GAO analysis of CDFI Fund Data. | GAO-14-500.

Figure 5. Number of Projects by Total Retentions and Fees Charged as a Percentage of Total New Markets Tax Credit (NMTC) Investment, 2011-2012.

Data on NMTC Equity Remaining in the Low-Income Community Businesses Are Not Sufficiently Complete or Accurate

Projects that have considerable equity are more likely to have better loan-to-value ratios and are generally more likely to obtain loans with better terms than projects without their own equity. For this reason, the larger the amount of equity remaining in the project, the greater is the likelihood that the project will continue on its own without any further government subsidies. However, the data available from the CDFI Fund reflect only the equity left by NMTC investors and may not give a complete picture of the economic viability of the business because it does not include other forms of equity, such as those from retained earnings for a successful business. Furthermore, the CDFI data on equity left in the business are not sufficiently reliable because they are incomplete and not accurate enough to capture program performance. According to our standards for measuring program performance, several elements should be considered when examining the quality of agency performance data including accuracy and completeness.

However, our review showed that about 60 percent of projects originating in 2011-2012 had inconsistencies that made these data unreliable. Examples of these inconsistencies are:

- **Incomplete data:** One or more CDEs involved in the project did not report any values making it impossible to calculate an amount for the entire project.
- **Inaccurate data:** Equity remaining was projected to equal or exceed 100 percent of all NMTC investments in the project. These amounts are not valid because they exceed the amounts of the original equity loan.
- **Zero values:** Some CDEs may be reporting a zero value because they do not intend to leave equity in the project. But according to CDFI Fund officials, other CDEs may intend to leave equity in the project, but reported zero value for accounting reasons because the charge would not be recorded until a later date. Thus, the zero values may be understating the equity available to the low-income community businesses.

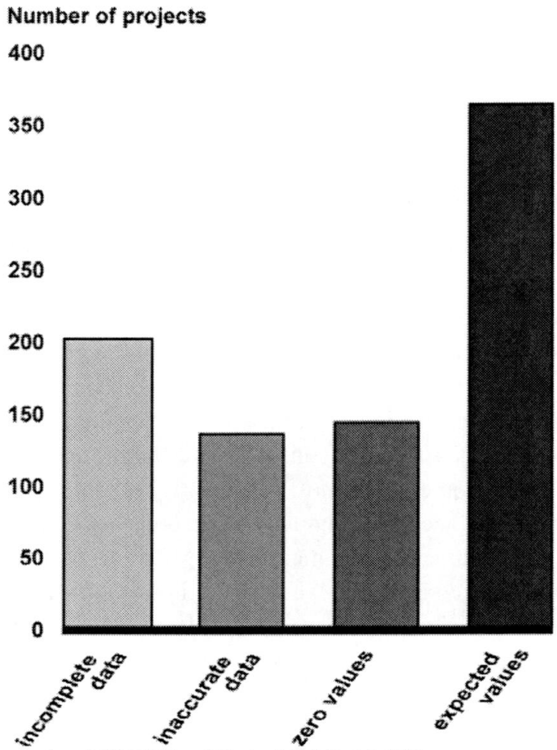

Source: GAO analysis of CDFI Fund Data. | GAO-14-500.

Note: CDFI Fund does not require data on equity remaining for any loans of investments originating before December 31, 2010. The figure is based on 842 projects with loans or investments originating in 2011-2012, the most recent available data.

Figure 6. Data Quality for Amounts of Equity Projected to Remain in the Low- Income Community Businesses, 2011-2012.

We determined that one cause of data unreliability was the unclear instructions in the manual for entering data into the CDFI Fund's systems. The manual does not clearly explain the time period for which information should be reported, which may have led to the CDEs reporting according to different accounting rules. Incomplete and inaccurate data result in an inability to use the data to track an important indicator of the likely performance of the NMTC projects after the compliance period ends. As a result, it is not possible to determine from these data the amount of equity to remain in the low-income community businesses after the 7-year credit period.

CDFI Fund Data on Distressed Projects Are Not Sufficiently Reliable

CDFI Fund data on projects experiencing financial distress, such as the number of days a loan is delinquent, track program performance in that they indicate how likely a project is to continue in business during and after the credit period. These indicators of financial distress must be weighed against other NMTC program goals. Another program goal is to encourage investors to invest in projects that may be more risky because they are located in low-income communities. Regardless, reliable performance data are needed to administer the program.

Our review of CDFI Fund data on the current status and performance of loans to NMTC projects showed inconsistencies that made these data not sufficiently reliable to determine the number and extent of projects experiencing financial distress. Examples of these inconsistencies include:

- **Incomplete data:** Ninety-nine percent of projects reported current loan status (a mandatory field), but approximately 30 percent of projects omitted additional information for the other potential indicators of distress such as the number of times a loan has been restructured, the number of days the loan is currently delinquent, and the dollar amount of any loan that has been charged off (optional or conditionally-required fields).
- **Inaccurate data:** Potential inaccuracies appear when we compared CDEs' descriptions of troubled projects from their NMTC allocation applications with indicators of distress for those same projects in CDFI Fund databases. In their 2012 applications, CDEs described 193 projects with delinquent, defaulted, or impaired loans in sufficient detail that we could identify those projects in the CDFI Fund data. But 49 of these projects showed no indications of distress in the data.

The causes of data unreliability were unclear instructions and optional reporting. CDEs enter their data into the CDFI Fund's electronic database. How they enter the data is determined by instructions provided by the CDFI Fund. We found a lack of clarity in these instructions that prevented us from being confident that the data provided an accurate measure of distress. For example, the instructions did not clearly distinguish restructured loans from refinanced loans. However, refinancing may not be an indicator of distress. It can occur for a variety of economic reasons. In addition, the data were incomplete because reporting some information was optional. Without accurate and complete data, the CDFI Fund does not have sufficient information to track program performance related to the future viability of the NMTC funded projects. CDFI Fund officials told us that they are changing all the loan performance data points to make them mandatory.

Difficulties in Determining Whether or Not a Project Has Failed

Project failures could significantly affect program performance by limiting its social and economic outcomes in low-income communities. However, determining when a project has failed is difficult. Projects that seem to be in difficulty based on the indicators of financial distress can become financially sound again. Some CDEs in their 2012 applications described successful restructurings of projects experiencing financial difficulty. But other projects are in situations where recovery seems unlikely or the CDEs have in fact written off the projects (see text boxes 1 and 2 for details of examples of both types of outcomes).

The CDFI Fund is developing additional tools to collect better information on failed projects. As discussed above, their current measures of financial distress are inaccurate or incomplete. However, even if the data are improved, the financial distress measures may not accurately identify project failures because the projects can recover from distress. The CDFI Fund is attempting to rectify this measurement problem with a close-out report which is intended to collect additional information on the status of the business at the end of the 7-year compliance period, such as whether a business continues to operate or a real estate project has been put into service.

Examples Illustrating Difficulties in Determining if a Project Has Failed

Text Box 1: Meat Processing Plant Investment That Failed

- An $8 million NMTC investment in a meat processing company involving two loans and one equity investment from one CDE.

- According to news accounts, the investments were needed to address liquidity problems created by an expansion of this ongoing business that employed about 300 people.
- According to the CDE's 2012 reapplication, the investments became impaired soon after the CDE made the investments when the leveraged lender limited the company's ability to borrow from its credit line, which forced the company into bankruptcy.
- The CDE unsuccessfully sought alternative financing for the company but still suffered a loss of $5.2 million.
- In the CDFI Fund data, one loan and one equity investment are reported as "charged off" for the full dollar amounts. The other loan is reported as "closed" but no amount charged off.

Source: GAO analysis of CDFI Fund data and public sources. | GAO-14-500

TEXT BOX 2: TROUBLED COLLEGE CONSTRUCTION PROJECT THAT RECOVERED

- A college construction project involving three CDEs and several NMTC loans.
- In their 2012 reapplications for NMTC allocations, two of the CDEs reported that their loans for the project became delinquent for as much as 480 days because of construction delays and the economic recession of 2008.
- The two CDEs reported that they worked with the borrower to rebalance the budget and bring in additional sources of financing.
- At the time of their applications, the two CDEs reported that all the previous interest was paid and all subsequent interest payments had been on time.
- The loans from the two CDEs show indications of poor performance (periods of delinquency) in CDFI Fund data.
- The third CDE did not report any delinquent or impaired loans in its 2012 reapplication, and its loans do not show any indications of poor performance in CDFI Fund data.

Source: GAO analysis of CDFI Fund data. | GAO-14-500.

Conclusion

The potential impact of the NMTC in promoting economic development in designated low-income communities is diluted if the NMTC provides an above-market rate of return. Similarly, the impact of a combination of assistance from government programs is diluted if in the same cases the combination of assistance is unnecessarily duplicative. Treasury guidance and controls that are designed to limit these risks can help ensure the NMTC program realizes the greatest possible impact on low- income communities.

Complete and reliable information is a vital component of assessing program effectiveness. While the complexity of the NMTC financial structures makes gathering information a challenge, there are several aspects of these structures where better information would aid in understanding the effectiveness of the program. These include the extent to which fees, interest rates, and other costs reduce the NMTC equity flowing to low-income community businesses, the amount of equity available to the low-income community businesses at the end of the 7-year compliance period, and the number of projects that failed or are at risk of failing.

Recommendations for Executive Action

We recommend that the Secretary of the Treasury take the following actions:

- Issue guidance on how funding or assistance from other government programs can be combined with the NMTC including the extent to which other government funds can be used to leverage the NMTC by being included in the qualified equity investment.
- Ensure that controls are in place to limit the risk of unnecessary duplication at the project level in funding or assistance from government programs and to limit above market rates of return, i.e., returns that are not commensurate with the NMTC investor's risk.
- Ensure that the CDFI Fund reviews the disclosure sheet that CDEs are required to provide to low-income community businesses to determine whether it contains data that could be useful for the Fund to retain.

- Ensure that the CDFI Fund clarifies the instructions for reporting the amount of any equity which may be acquired by the low-income community business at the end of the 7-year NMTC compliance period.
- Ensure that the CDFI Fund clarifies the instructions it provides to CDEs about reporting loan performance and make the reporting of that data mandatory.

AGENCY COMMENTS AND OUR EVALUATION

We provided a draft of this product to Treasury for comment on June 11, 2014. In its written comments, Treasury concurred with two of our recommendations and reported that the other recommendations are under consideration. The CDFI Fund also provided technical comments that were incorporated, as appropriate.

Treasury said that it is considering our recommendations to issue further guidance on how other government programs can be combined with NMTCs, and to ensure that adequate controls are in place to limit the risks of unnecessary duplication and above-market rates of return. Treasury reported that our recommendations would be reviewed in consultation with a recently formed working group that includes representatives from the IRS and the CDFI Fund to discuss potential administrative or regulatory changes.

Treasury said that it is considering our recommendation about reviewing data presented in the disclosure sheets that CDEs are required to provide low-income community businesses. As our report states, not all information on the disclosure sheets, such as third-party transactions costs, is reported to the CDFI Fund. This additional information on the disclosure sheets could be useful for the CDFI Fund to retain.

Treasury agreed with our recommendation to clarify instructions for reporting any equity amounts that may be acquired by the low-income community business at the end of the compliance period. Treasury also agreed with our recommendation to clarify instructions to CDEs about reporting loan performance and make this data reporting mandatory.

Sincerely yours,
James R. White
Director, Tax Issues
Strategic Issues

APPENDIX I. OBJECTIVES, SCOPE, AND METHODOLOGY

The objectives of this report were to assess: (1) New Markets Tax Credit (NMTC) financial structures in terms of their complexity, transparency, and effect on the size of the federal subsidies going to NMTC projects as well as controls to ensure that subsidies are not larger than necessary for the investment; (2) what is known about the types and amounts of fees and other costs that reduce the amount of equity reaching low-income community businesses; (3) what is known about the amount of equity left in the low-income community businesses after the 7-year credit period; and (4) what is known about NMTC projects that are at risk of failing by becoming economically nonviable.

For our first objective, we reviewed the NMTC literature and interviewed representatives of community development entities (CDEs) and researchers who have evaluated the program to determine how the financial structures have evolved. To assess the complexity and transparency of NMTC investment structures, we applied criteria from our prior work on evaluating tax expenditures.[17] We also applied criteria from federal government internal control standards to assess whether controls are present to ensure that subsidies are not larger than necessary for a NMTC project.[18]

To report on the number, types, and funding amounts of other federal programs used on NMTC projects, we designed and implemented a web-based survey to gather information on how projects were financed from the CDEs responsible for the project. Our survey population consisted of randomly selected NMTC projects with all loans and investments closing on or after January 1, 2010. Restricting the survey population to NMTC projects within our study's time period left us with a total of 1,265 projects in the population. We selected a stratified sample of 305 projects. From the first strata, defined as those projects for which there is an indication on the underlying population file that at least one of the funding sources was public dollars, we selected 126 projects. From the second strata, defined as all other projects, we selected 179 projects. Although some projects in the second strata could actually have public dollars, this stratification helps ensure that our sample has enough of these cases to produce estimates of that domain.

The survey asked the CDEs a combination of questions that allowed for open-ended and close-ended responses with regard to federal, state, local, and private funding sources. We pre-tested the content and format of the questionnaire with four knowledgeable CDEs and made changes based on pretest results. The survey was a web-based survey. We sent an activation e-mail for the survey on March 7, 2014, and closed the survey on April 4, 2014.

The practical difficulties of conducting any survey may introduce errors, commonly referred to as non-sampling errors. For example, differences in how a particular question is interpreted, the sources of information available to respondents, how the responses were processed and analyzed, or the types of people who do not respond can influence the accuracy of the survey results. We took steps in the development of the survey, the data collection, and the data analysis to minimize these non- sampling errors and help ensure the accuracy of the answers that were obtained. A second independent analyst checked all the computer programs that processed the data. In instances where multiple CDEs responded about the same project, we manually merged the data together into a representative single project following the Community Development Financial Institutions (CDFI) Fund's practices, such as reporting the highest value as the default estimate.

We obtained responses for 214 of the 305 projects in our sample for an overall response rate of about 70 percent. Population estimates were produced by weighting the sample data from the responding projects to account for differing sampling rates for projects funded with public dollars and those funded without public dollars. We have treated the respondents as a stratified random sample and calculated sampling errors as an estimate of the uncertainty around the survey estimates. All percentage estimates based on this sample have 95 percent confidence intervals of within +/- 7 percentage points of the estimate itself. For other numeric estimates, the 95 percent confidence intervals are presented along with the estimates themselves. We are 95 percent confident that each of the confidence intervals in this report will include the true values in the study population.

To address the last three objectives, we analyzed data from the CDFI Fund on NMTC investments in low-income community businesses from 2003 through 2012. The CDFI Fund requires all CDEs that have been awarded NMTC allocations to submit an annual report detailing how they invested the qualified equity investment (QEI) proceeds in low-income communities. These reports must be submitted to the CDFI Fund by the CDEs, along with their audited financial statements, within 6 months after the end of their fiscal years. CDEs are required to report their NMTC investments in the CDFI Fund's Community Investment Impact System (CIIS) for a period of 7 years. Due to a time lag in reporting, NMTC investments reported in CIIS are less than the total amount allocated for the NMTC program.[19] Given that the CDFI Fund requires CDEs to report information on project characteristics and financing once a year, CIIS data may not capture the most current information for all existing projects. However, the CIIS data that we used represent the most current available information as of December 2, 2013 on the status of the program. We interviewed CDFI Fund officials with knowledge of CIIS about the steps they take to ensure its accuracy. Based on GAO's criteria for valid data— that they be sufficiently accurate and complete to capture program performance—we also determined the data on fees and retentions we used in this report were sufficiently reliable for our purposes (see below for discussion of the data we found unreliable for our purposes).[20]

To describe the types and amounts of fees and other costs, we analyzed data that CDEs reported to the CDFI Fund on the NMTC investment proceeds they retained and fees they charged to investors, low-income community businesses, and others. We analyzed the fee data at the project level for 794 projects with loans and investments originating in 2011 and 2012. The CDFI Fund began requiring that CDEs report data on QEI proceeds that the CDEs retained and their other fees starting with the 2011 reporting period, and only for loans and investments originating after December 31, 2010.[21] We used fees data reported in basis points and data on the qualified low-income community investment (QLICI) amounts to calculate the total dollar amounts of fees. We compared our final results to other data on fees submitted by CDEs when applying for NMTC allocations in 2010 and 2011.

We attempted to compare these costs to costs on non-NMTC investments by reviewing industry data and academic studies on fees, and interviewing industry and tax credit experts. We also reviewed written and oral comments made by CDEs and industry experts to the CDFI Fund in response to a November 7, 2011, *Federal Register* notice soliciting comments on several possible NMTC program changes. The CDFI Fund specifically requested comments on whether additional rules, restrictions, and requirements should be imposed related to fees and expenses charged by CDEs. The CDFI Fund also held three listening sessions in December 2012 and January and February 2013 with a total of 45 CDE and industry experts. We reviewed the transcripts of these listening sessions and concluded from these reviews that the types of projects funded by the NMTC are so varied that we could not conduct a valid comparison of fee costs with those on non-NMTC projects.

We attempted to determine the amount of equity that remains in low-income community businesses by analyzing data reported by CDEs to the CDFI Fund on equity projected to remain in NMTC projects at the end of the 7-year credit period. We analyzed these data at the project level for 842 projects with loans and investments originating in 2011 and 2012. Starting with the 2011 reporting period, the CDFI Fund began requiring that, if applicable, CDEs report the projected amount of any equity or debt investment which may be acquired by the low-income community business as the result of a put/call option or other arrangement for loans and investments originating after December 31, 2010. After reviewing all 2,249 transactions for all 842 projects, we determined that data were usable for only 363 projects (about 40 percent), and therefore the data could not be used to give sufficiently reliable descriptions of the equity remaining in the project for our purposes. We found the following problems with the data that made the values unreliable for our report.

- For 201 projects, no data were reported by one or more of the CDEs involved in those projects. We concluded that in these cases we could not determine: (1) how many of these projects were non-leveraged where the failure to project a residual value might be expected; (2) how many indicated a true intention not to leave any equity in the project; and (3) how many were simply errors or omissions.
- For another 143 projects, one or more CDEs involved reported a total projected residual value of $0. We concluded in these cases that the implications of zero for equity remaining were ambiguous. According CFDI Fund officials, some CDEs may in fact do not intend to leave any residual equity for the business to obtain at the end of the 7-year period. However, other CDEs may project $0 remaining now when in fact they intend to designate the amount of equity at a later date. These CDEs may be reporting a zero value at this time due to an individual CDE's internal practices or accounting rules particular to the CDE's form of incorporation. That is, the CDEs would not report a projected or final residual value until the put/call option was exercised by the business.
- Of the remaining 498 projects, 135 projects had data showing that the total projected residual value for these projects appeared to be overstated. Some data showed that one or more CDEs reported projected residual values greater than or equal to the original equity investment values. In most of these cases, the CDEs appeared to have incorrectly reported a projected residual value for both leveraged loans and equity investments. Based on the typical leveraged model structure, the CDEs should have only reported the residual value of the equity investments. In other cases, one or more CDEs involved in a project reported the projected residual value of the equity

investment twice—once as value for the equity investment, and then repeated it as a value for the leveraged loan. As a result of these reporting errors or inconsistencies, the total projected residual value for these projects appeared to be overstated.

To determine the NMTC projects at risk of failing by becoming economically nonviable, we analyzed data reported by CDEs to the CDFI Fund that could indicate that a project is experiencing financial distress. We used indicators of financial distress that are available from CDFI Fund data, such as whether a loan on a project is delinquent, charged off, or restructured that could show increased risk of business failure. These indicators, in most cases, could not be used to conclude that a business has failed in the sense of being economically nonviable as the CDFI Fund does not currently have data on the ultimate disposition of NMTC projects. We analyzed the number of projects that showed indications of financial distress between 2003 and 2012, and the dollar amounts invested in these financially distressed projects. We tested the reliability of these optional fields by reviewing CDEs applications for 2012 NMTC allocations. In the application instructions, CDEs were asked to discuss any delinquent, defaulted, or impaired loans or equity investments from prior NMTC investments. In the 2012 applications, we counted 281 projects with delinquent, defaulted, or impaired loans or investments. Of these, 193 projects were described in sufficient detail that we could then match those projects to transaction-level data in CIIS. However, 49 of those projects did not show any indications of financial distress in CIIS. For some projects involving multiple CDEs, one or more CDEs may have described the project in their 2012 applications as having delinquent, defaulted, or impaired investments, but only one CDE then reported any of the optional distress indicator data in CIIS. In other cases, CDEs described several projects in the 2012 applications as having delinquent, defaulted, or impaired investments, but then those CDEs did not report any distress indicators for these projects in CIIS. In the end, we concluded that the CDFI Fund CIIS data on indicators of financial distress were insufficient for our purposes, largely due to the fact that nearly all of the distress indicators were optional data fields. We conducted this performance audit from May 2013 to July 2014 in accordance with generally accepted government auditing standards. Those standards require that we plan and perform the audit to obtain sufficient, appropriate evidence to provide a reasonable basis for our findings and conclusions based on our audit objectives. We believe that the evidence obtained provides a reasonable basis for our findings and conclusions based on our audit objectives.

Appendix II. Other Federal Funding Used in New Markets Tax Credit Projects

In our survey of New Markets Tax Credit (NMTC) projects, we asked Community Development Entities (CDEs) what other federal sources of assistance were used (in addition to the NMTC) to fund the project.[22] CDEs could select from a pre-populated list of federal sources comprised of federal tax credits, public bond financing exempt from federal tax, grants or direct payments from federal agencies, and direct or guaranteed loans from federal agencies. Our survey also permitted CDEs to write in other federal sources not included in the pre-populated list. CDEs were also asked if the NMTC was "twinned" or "enhanced" with any of these federal sources inside the NMTC structure, i.e., did NMTC investors claim NMTCs based on these additional amounts of federal assistance. The NMTC investor community often refers to this practice as "twinning" the NMTC with other tax credits or other public assistance, but for purposes of this report, we define this as leveraging other public sources with the NMTC. The four tables below list the types of other federal assistance (from our pre-populated list of federal assistance and write-in descriptions) that CDEs reported as being used to finance our sample of NMTC projects, and whether these other federal sources were leveraged with the NMTC.

Table 4. Other Federal Tax Credits Used in a Sample of New Markets Tax Credit (NMTC) Projects, 2010-2012

	Federal source was leveraged with NMTC one or more times
10 percent credit for rehabilitation of structures (other than historic)	
20 percent credit for rehabilitation of historic structures (Historic Tax Credit)	yes
Business Energy Investment Tax Credit (ITC)	yes
Credit for qualified school construction bonds	yes
Brownfield credits	

Source: GAO survey of NMTC projects originating in 2010-2012. | GAO-14-500

Table 5. Tax Exempt Bond Financing Used in a Sample of New Markets Tax Credit (NMTC) Projects, 2010-2012

	Federal source was leveraged with NMTC one or more times
Exclusion of interest for airport, dock, and similar bonds	
Exclusion of interest on bonds for private nonprofit educational facilities	yes
Exclusion of interest on bonds for private nonprofit hospital facilities	yes
Exclusion of interest on Gulf Opportunity Zone Revenue Bonds	
Exclusion of interest on Recovery Zone Bonds	yes
Federal Energy 179D (tax deduction)	
Various public purpose state and local bonds[a]	yes

Source: GAO survey of NMTC projects originating in 2010-2012. | GAO-14-500

[a] A number of survey respondents indicated receiving project financing from a variety of state and locally-issued bonds.

Table 6. Grants or Direct Payments Used in a Sample of New Markets Tax Credit (NMTC) Projects, 2010-2012

	Federal source was leveraged with NMTC one or more times
Department of Housing and Urban Development (HUD)	
Community Development Block Grants/Entitlement Grants (CDBG)	yes
HUD Economic Development Initiative	
HUD Financial Grant	
HUD Capital Fund Education and Training Community Facilities Program	yes
Neighborhood Stabilization Program (NSP)	yes
Public Housing Development Funds	yes
Department of Energy	
Energy Efficiency and Conservation Block Grant (EECBG)	

	Federal source was leveraged with NMTC one or more times
Department of Health and Human Services	
Grants to Health Center Programs	yes
Office of Head Start (OHS)	
Department of the Treasury	
1603 Program: Payments for Specified Energy Property in Lieu of Tax Credits	
U.S. Treasury - Neighbor Works	
Department of Education	
Impact Aid grant	yes
Department of Education unspecified grant	
Department of Defense	
Department of Defense unspecified grant	
Environmental Protection Agency(EPA)	
EPA Grant	
Federal Communications Commission (FCC)	
FCC Grants for Rural Healthcare	
Federal Home Loan Bank	
Federal Home Loan Bank grants	
Department of Veterans Affairs(VA)	
VA tenant improvement payment	
Unspecified	
Rural Community Assistance Partnership (RCAP)	
American Recovery Reinvestment Act (ARRA)	

Source: GAO survey of NMTC projects originating in 2010-2012. | GAO-14-500

Table 7. Direct Loans or Guaranteed Loans Used in a Sample of New Markets Tax Credit (NMTC) Projects, 2010-2012

	Federal source was leveraged with NMTC one or more times
Department of Agriculture	
Business and Industry Loans	

Table 7. (Continued)

	Federal source was leveraged with NMTC one or more times
Community Facilities Loans	
Department of Housing and Urban Development	
Section 108 Community Development Loan Guarantees	
Supplemental Loan Insurance Multifamily Rental Housing	
Small Business Administration (SBA)	
SBA 7(a) Guaranteed Loan	
SBA 504 loan program	
SBA unspecified guaranteed loan	
Department of Education	
Charter School Credit Enhancement Grant	
Department of Energy	
ARRA Energy Loan Program—Green Energy Loan Fund	
Other	
Department of Housing and Community Development (state) CDBG-ARRA	yes

Source: GAO survey of NMTC projects originating in 2010-2012. | GAO-14-500

Appendix III. Regression Analysis of Total Fees and Retentions Associated with Characteristics of the Project Using CDFI Fund Data, 2011-2012

Variable Name	Coefficient	Std. Error	t	P>|t|
Average interest rate on loans	.0968962	.0360374	2.69	0.007
Dollar amount of NMTC qualified equity investment (QEI)	.0782438	.0014382	54.40	0.000
Number of transactions (financial structure complexity)	.0482567	.0189266	2.55	0.011
Poverty rate > 30% (distressed community)	-.302405	.1086737	-2.78	0.005
Dollar amount of non-public funds used on project	-.0009428	.0002418	-3.90	0.000
Purpose: business	.2869305	.1392813	2.12	0.040

Variable Name	Coefficient	Std. Error	t	P>|t|
Purpose: construction	-.0928775	.1401169	-0.66	0.507
Origination year: 2012	-.1675759	.1076841	-1.56	0.120
Constant	-.5996888	.1900319	-3.16	0.002

Source: GAO analysis of CDFI Fund data. | GAO-14-500

Notes: N=2,018; R-squared = 0.6028. Dollar amounts are scaled in $100,000 units.

The table reports the results of an ordinary least squares regression with the dependent variable equal to the amount of fees and retentions charged. Omitted category variables are: project type equal to "rehabilitation or other" and origination year equal to "2011." The regression was also estimated using various functional forms including quadratic and log forms of the regression equation. These specifications either were rejected as statistically insignificant or, in the case of some of the log specifications, resulted in a substantial decrease in the explanatory power of the regression as measured by its R-squared.

This regression was also estimated with fees and retentions as separate dependent variables, and, in these cases, the results were different for certain variables of interest. With fees as the dependent variable, neither the interest rate nor the number of transactions was statistically significant at the 95 percent confidence level. However, the size of the qualified equity investment remained positive and significant. With retentions as the dependent variable, the retentions were positively and significantly related to interest rates but had no statistically significant relationship to the number of transactions.

End Notes

[1] Pub. L. No.106-554, § 121, 114 Stat. 2763 (2000) *codified at* 26 U.S.C. § 45D.

[2] See list of related GAO products at the end of this report.

[3] For more detail on these criteria, see GAO, *Tax Expenditures: Background and Evaluation Criteria and Questions*, GAO-13-167SP (Washington, D.C.: Nov. 29, 2012); GAO, *Understanding the Tax Reform Debate: Background, Criteria and Questions*, GAO-05-1009SP (Washington, D.C.: Sept. 1, 2005); and GAO, *Standards for Internal Control in the Federal Government,* GAO/AIMD-00-21.3.1 (Washington, D.C.: Nov. 1, 1999).

[4] All estimates based on our survey are subject to sampling error. For percentage estimates, the 95 percent confidence intervals are within +/- 7 percentage points of the estimate itself.

[5] GAO, *New Markets Tax Credit: The Credit Helps Fund a Variety of Projects in Low- Income Communities, but Could Be Simplified,* GAO-10-334 (Washington, D.C.: Jan. 29, 2010).

[6] At the time of this report's publication, there are many bills pending in Congress that would extend the expired NMTC. For example, the Senate had begun floor debate on S.2260,

which would extend the NMTC through 2015. The House of Representatives had yet not begun considering H.R.3939 or H.R.4365, which would permanently extend the credit.

[7] For a discussion of the criteria appropriate for evaluating tax expenditures such as the NMTC, see GAO, *Tax Expenditures: Background and Evaluation Criteria and Questions,* GAO-13-167SP (Washington, D.C.: Nov. 29, 2012).

[8] The simplified examples focus on the revenue effects of the NMTC and are not intended to be estimates of the credit's total revenue cost. For example, they do not reflect other tax liabilities that investors may incur on the credit claimed that would reduce the revenue cost. For estimates of NMTC revenue costs, see U.S. Congress Joint Committee on Taxation, *Estimated Revenue Effects of the Revenue Provisions Contained in the "Family and Business Tax Cut Certainty Act of 2012," as reported by the Senate Committee on Finance,* Aug. 29, 2012, JCX-71-12.

[9] In Rev. Rul. 2003-20, the IRS ruled that for purposes of determining the NMTC allowable under Section 45D, the amount of the QEI made by an investment fund may include cash from a nonrecourse loan that the investment fund invests as equity in a qualified CDE. In Rev. Rul. 2010-17, the IRS ruled that the amount of QEI could also include cash from a recourse loan.

[10] In Notice 2002-64, IRS allowed the NMTC to be combined with other federal programs except the Low-Income Housing Tax Credit (LIHTC). Treasury issued final regulations in 2004 incorporating the guidance from the 2002 IRS Notice—see Treas. Reg. § 1.45D-1(g)(3). Investors interpreted the Treasury regulations, together with the 2003 Revenue Ruling allowing leveraging of private debt, to permit leveraging with other federal programs such as historic tax credits where the value of these credits was used to increase the base of the NMTC by being loaned to an investment fund. Treasury has not amended its regulations or issued specific guidance to address this practice.

[11] GAO, *Tax Policy: New Markets Tax Credit Appears to Increase Investment by Investors in Low-Income Communities, but Opportunities Exist to Better Monitor Compliance,* GAO-07-296 (Washington, D.C.: Jan. 31, 2007); and New Markets Tax Credit Coalition, *New Markets Tax Credit Progress Report 2014,* (Washington, D.C.: June 10, 2014).

[12] According to data from an accounting and consulting firm, 15 states currently have state new markets tax credit programs and 36 states have state historic tax credit programs. Novogradac & Company LLP, *Tax Credit Resource Centers,* accessed June 10, 2014, http://www.novoco.com/resource_center/index.php.

[13] Urban Institute, *New Markets Tax Credit (NMTC) Program Evaluation: Final Report,* a report prepared for U.S. Department of the Treasury, Community Development Financial Institutions (CDFI) Fund, April 2013.

[14] 26 U.S.C. § 45D(i)(1); Treas. Reg. § 1.45D-1(g)(3).

[15] These risks of higher costs led, in part, to our prior suggestion that Congress consider a pilot test whereby some NMTCs would be converted to grants.

[16] As part of their 2012 NMTC Allocation Agreements with the CDFI Fund, CDEs are now required to prepare a separate stand-alone document that discloses "any and all direct and indirect" NMTC-related transactions costs related to the loan or investment (such as third-party legal and accounting costs), and any compensation (fees) that the CDE is assessing the low-income community business prior, to, during, and at the conclusion of the 7-year NMTC term. The CDFI Fund provided a sample disclosure statement to CDEs based on commonly-used leverage model transactions and typical costs identified with NMTC transactions. The CDEs are required to provide the low-income community businesses a final disclosure statement at closing.

[17] GAO, *Tax Expenditures: Background and Evaluation Criteria and Questions,* GAO-13-167SP (Washington, D.C.: Nov. 29, 2012) and *Understanding the Tax Reform Debate: Background, Criteria and Questions*, GAO-05-1009SP (Washington, D.C.: Sept. 1, 2005).

[18] GAO, *Standards for Internal Control in the Federal Government,* GAO/AIMD-00-21.3.1 (Washington, D.C.: Nov. 1, 1999).

[19] U.S. Department of the Treasury, Community Development Financial Institutions Fund, "New Markets Tax Credit Public Data Release: 2003-2011 Summary Report," July 2, 2013.

[20] GAO, *Managing for Results: Assessing the Quality of Program Performance Data*, GAO/GGD-00-140R, (Washington, D.C.: May 25, 2000).

[21] Seventy-three projects were excluded because they had loans and investments originating both before and after December 31, 2010, and 49 projects were excluded because one or more CDEs appeared to have reported fees data incorrectly by reporting fees as a percentage of the QEI rather than as basis points as instructed by the CDFI Fund.

[22] As noted in appendix I, our survey population consisted of randomly selected NMTC projects with all loans and investments closing on or after January 1, 2010. Restricting the survey population to NMTC projects within our study's time period left us with a total of 1,265 projects in the starting population from which we drew our sample.

In: The New Markets Tax Credit
Editor: Marlin Barrett
ISBN: 978-1-63463-644-5

Chapter 4

NEW MARKETS TAX CREDIT: THE CREDIT HELPS FUND A VARIETY OF PROJECTS IN LOW-INCOME COMMUNITIES, BUT COULD BE SIMPLIFIED*

United States Government Accountability Office

WHY GAO DID THIS STUDY

The Treasury Department's Community Development Financial Institutions (CDFI) Fund awarded $26 billion in New Markets Tax Credits (NMTC) through 2009 for investment in low-income communities. The NMTC allows investors to claim a tax credit totaling 39 percent of their investment in Community Development Entities (CDE) over 7 years which CDEs reinvest in qualified communities.

This mandated report (1) describes where and how CDEs are using NMTCs, (2) assesses how CDEs use NMTCs to offer favorable financing terms to low-income community businesses and describes options for simplifying the NMTC, (3) describes how, if at all, NMTC investments support low-income community development, and (4) determines how effective IRS and the CDFI Fund have been in monitoring NMTC compliance.

* This is an edited, reformatted and augmented version of a United States Government Accountability Office publication, No. GAO-10-334, dated January 2010.

GAO analyzed CDFI Fund and CDE data, did case studies of CDEs, and interviewed relevant experts.

WHAT GAO RECOMMENDS

Congress should consider options to simplify the NMTC's structure, and GAO recommends that the Secretary of the Treasury direct the CDFI Fund Director to collect additional data on program performance and improve project-level data. The CDFI Fund agreed with GAO's recommendations and disagreed with GAO's matter for Congress. GAO maintained its matter for Congress; evaluating the simplification's effects can include the Fund's concerns.

WHAT GAO FOUND

Since 2003, CDEs have made NMTC investments in all 50 states, the District of Columbia, and Puerto Rico, with about 65 percent for real estate. NMTCs are often used as "gap financing," accounting for a portion of total project costs.

NMTC investments in low-income community businesses generally use leveraged structures, where equity is left in the businesses, or subsidized interest rate structures, where below-market interest rate loans are offered. Recently, investors appear to be paying less for tax credits than in previous years and they made fewer NMTC investments in 2009 than in previous years. The CDFI Fund does not collect data that could identify the portion of the subsidy channeled to businesses, such as data on credit pricing, transaction fees, and the amount of equity left in businesses. Two potential options (i.e., changing related parties tests or converting the NMTC to a grant program) could simplify the program and make additional funds available to businesses.

CDEs have used the NMTC program to support a variety of investments, but project impacts are difficult to measure and likely vary depending on the project. GAO identified NMTC-supported projects for mixed-use facilities, housing developments, and community facilities, among other qualified business activities. The CDFI Fund does not collect data on incomplete or failed projects, which might be used, for instance, to improve credit allocation selections. Projects with NMTC financing likely contribute employment and other outcomes to low-income communities. Limitations with available data make it difficult to isolate project impacts and GAO's analysis does not allow it to determine whether the projects supported by NMTCs would have taken place absent the credit. Continued improvements could be made in collecting project-level data (e.g., removing double-counting of some outcomes).

IRS monitors CDE and investor compliance with applicable laws, while the CDFI Fund monitors CDEs' compliance with their allocation agreements. IRS and CDFI Fund officials weighed the costs and benefits of options to monitor compliance and selected controls on that basis.

ABBREVIATIONS

AMT	Alternative Minimum Tax
CDE	Community Development Entity
CDFI	Community Development Financial Institutions
CIIS	Community Investment Impact System
FTE	Full-Time Equivalent
GO Zone	Gulf Opportunity Zone
HFA	Housing finance agency
IRS	Internal Revenue Service
LIHTC	Low-Income Housing Tax Credit
NCMS	New Markets Compliance Monitoring System
NMTC	New Markets Tax Credit
OMB	Office of Management and Budget
QALICB	Qualified active low-income community business
QEI	Qualified Equity Investment
QLICI	Qualified low-income community investment

* * *

January 29, 2010

Congressional Committees

Congress established the New Markets Tax Credit (NMTC) program as part of the Community Renewal Tax Relief Act of 2000[1] to encourage investors to make investments in impoverished, low-income communities that traditionally lack access to capital. Conventional access to credit and investment capital for developing small businesses, creating and retaining jobs, and revitalizing neighborhoods is often limited in economically distressed communities or in communities with large low-income populations. The NMTC provides investors (individuals, financial institutions, other corporations, etc.) with a tax credit for investing in communities that are economically distressed or consist of low-income populations.

The NMTC program is administered by the Community Development Financial Institutions (CDFI) Fund in the Department of The Treasury which allocates tax credit authority—the amount of investment which investors use as the base for determining the amount of tax credits they are eligible to claim—to Community Development Entities (CDE) that apply for and obtain allocations. As of January 2010, the CDFI Fund had allocated all $26 billion in total available NMTC allocation authority. The NMTC expired following the 2009 allocation round. However, legislative proposals have been put forth that would extend the program beyond 2009.

The Community Renewal Tax Relief Act of 2000 mandated that we report to Congress on the NMTC program by January 31, 2004, 2007, and 2010. In our report issued January 31, 2004, we described the status of the NMTC program, profiled CDEs that received first-round allocations, and evaluated whether systems were in place or planned to ensure NMTC compliance.[2] We concluded that progress was being made in implementing the program and recommended that the Internal Revenue Service (IRS) and the CDFI Fund work together to take additional steps toward monitoring compliance. In response, IRS and the CDFI Fund took steps to design and implement compliance monitoring processes. In our 2007 report, we reviewed whether the NMTC appeared to be generating new investment in low-income communities and revisited CDFI Fund and IRS efforts to monitor compliance.[3] We concluded that the NMTC appeared to be generating new investment from individual investors and that corporate investors appeared to be shifting investments from higher income areas to low-income communities. We also made recommendations to IRS to develop a representative sample of CDEs to select for a compliance study and to explore options for cost-effectively monitoring investor compliance. In response, IRS used CDFI Fund data to revise criteria for selecting a more representative sample of CDEs to review as part of its compliance study and IRS studied the feasibility of developing a comprehensive investor compliance program. IRS concluded that such a program would not be cost-effective and that currently available data should allow them to detect investor noncompliance. In addition to our two mandated reports, in the spring of 2009, we addressed congressional interest in minority

CDEs' NMTC participation rates and found that minority CDEs have not been as successful in obtaining allocations as nonminority CDEs.[4] The CDFI Fund generally agreed with the findings of our requested report on minority CDEs' participation in the NMTC program.

Based on consultations with your offices, this final mandated report: (1) describes where and how CDEs are using NMTCs to invest in low-income communities and targeted populations; (2) assesses how CDEs use NMTC financing to offer favorable financing terms to low-income community businesses and describes options for simplifying NMTC investment structures; (3) describes how, if at all, NMTC investments appear to support low-income community development; and (4) determines how effective measures taken by the CDFI Fund and the IRS have been in monitoring CDEs' and investors' compliance with the NMTC program.

To accomplish these objectives, we used multiple methods of analysis. We analyzed data from the CDFI Fund's Community Investment Impact System (CIIS) database that contains data on the status of NMTC projects through fiscal year 2008. We analyzed information obtained through a non-generalizable, purposeful sample of nine case study CDEs. To capture the range of projects supported by NMTC investment, we selected case study CDEs based on the geographic distribution of their operations, their communities of service (i.e., urban or rural), their status as a for-profit or nonprofit organization, and the asset size of a CDE or its parent corporation. We limited our CDE selection to organizations that received NMTC awards in the 2005 and 2006 allocation rounds, to examine NMTC investments that better reflect the types of investments that have taken place as the program has matured. In addition, we interviewed and analyzed information obtained from local lenders and other subject-matter experts who are familiar with the low-income communities, targeted populations, and businesses that the case study CDEs serve. We also met with officials from the CDFI Fund and IRS, and reviewed documents on their efforts to monitor NMTC compliance.

We interviewed CDFI Fund officials with knowledge of the CIIS about the steps they take to ensure its accuracy and reviewed the computer programs the CDFI Fund uses to generate its NMTC databases. We determined that the data in this report were sufficiently reliable for our purposes. We conducted this performance audit from September 2008 through January 2010 in accordance with generally accepted government auditing standards. Those standards require that we plan and perform the audit to obtain sufficient, appropriate evidence to provide a reasonable basis for our findings and conclusions based on our audit objectives.

We believe that the evidence obtained provides a reasonable basis for our findings and conclusions based on our audit objectives.

BACKGROUND

The CDFI Fund in the Department of The Treasury is authorized to allocate $26 billion[5] in tax credit authority to CDEs that manage NMTC investments in low-income community development projects.[6] Eligible organizations may apply for and receive NMTC allocations once they have been certified as a CDE by the CDFI Fund (a CDE that receives an allocation is often referred to as an allocatee).[7] Since the first round of NMTC allocations in 2003, demand for the NMTC has exceeded available allocation authority by at least 4.5 times in each allocation round. As of January 2010, the CDFI Fund had awarded all $26 billion in NMTC authority through 2009. The program expired at the end of 2009, but legislation has been proposed that would extend the program for future years.[8]

The NMTC Investment Process

As figure 1 illustrates, after the CDFI Fund makes allocations to CDEs, investors make qualified equity investments (QEI) by acquiring stock or a capital interest in the CDEs, and, in exchange, can claim tax credits on a portion of their investment. The CDEs, in turn, are required to invest “substantially all” of the proceeds they receive into qualified low-income community investments (QLICI).[9]

QLICI investments include (but are not limited to) investments in businesses, referred to as qualified active low-income community businesses (QALICB), to be used for residential, commercial and industrial projects, and other types of investments such as purchasing loans from other CDEs.

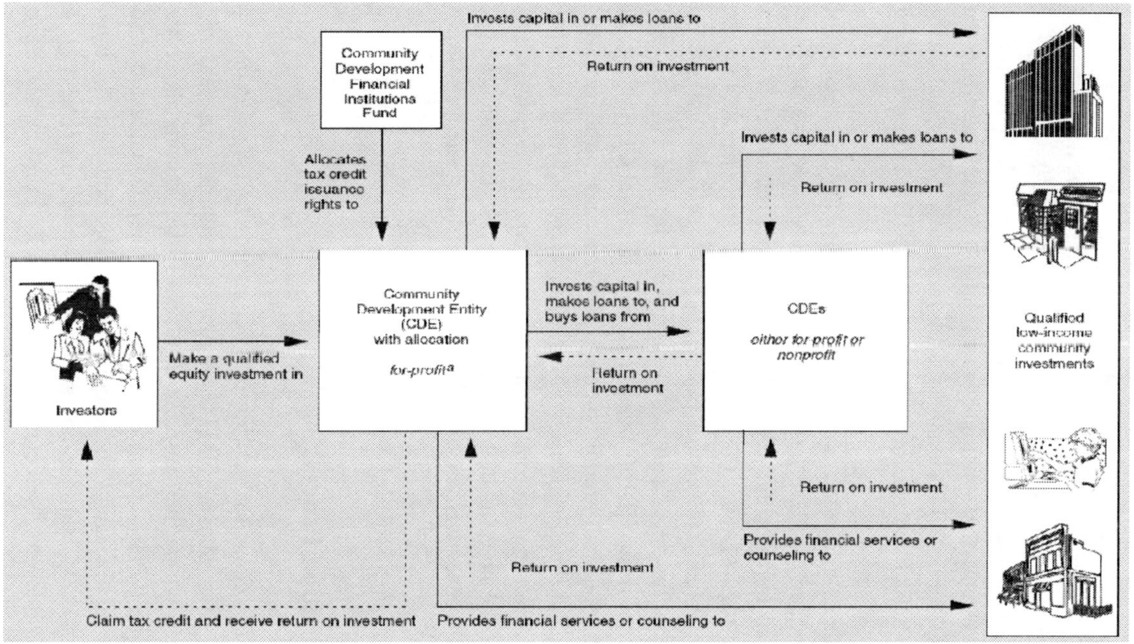

Source: GAO.

[a]Only a for-profit CDE can receive qualified equity investment from NMTC investors. These CDEs can then make investments in other CDEs that could be for-profit CDEs or nonprofit CDEs or they can directly invest the NMTC funds in low-income communities. However, both for-profit and nonprofit CDEs can receive allocations from the CDFI Fund. If a nonprofit CDE receives a NMTC allocation from the CDFI Fund, it must transfer the allocation authority to a for-profit CDE before NMTC investments can be made.

Figure 1. NMTC Process for Using Allocated Tax Credits to Make QLICIs.

Although for-profit and nonprofit CDEs can apply for and receive NMTC allocations, only for-profit CDEs can offer NMTCs to investors because, by definition, nonprofit organizations generally do not have access to equity investment. When a nonprofit CDE receives a NMTC allocation, it must transfer the allocation to one or more of its for-profit subsidiaries. The for-profit subsidiaries do not have to be formed when the nonprofit CDE applies for an allocation. However, the subsidiary must submit a CDE certification application to the CDFI Fund within 30 days of receiving a Notification of Allocation from the CDFI Fund and must be a certified CDE before entering into an allocation agreement.

Once a CDE with an allocation has obtained qualified equity investment from NMTC investors and the CDE has invested the funds in an eligible low-income community, an investor can claim NMTCs over a period of 7 years totaling 39 percent of their original QEI.[10] The NMTC is a nonrefundable tax credit, meaning taxpayers do not receive payments for tax credits that exceed their total tax liability. Investors can cease to qualify for the NMTC, and trigger a recapture event if the CDE (1) ceases to be a certified CDE, (2) does not satisfy the "substantially all" requirement, or (3) redeems the investment. A recapture event means that an investor will no longer be able to claim the credit, and that the investor that originally purchased the equity investment and subsequent holders of the investment are required to increase their income tax liability by the credits previously claimed plus interest for each resulting underpayment of tax.[11]

The NMTC Application Process

The CDFI Fund's process for making NMTC awards takes place in two phases. Under the first phase, NMTC applicants submit standardized application packages in which they respond to a series of questions about the CDE's track record, the dollar amount of allocated tax credits requested, and the organization's plans for using the credits to support activities in low-income communities. NMTC applications are first reviewed and scored by a group of external reviewers selected by the CDFI Fund who have demonstrated experience in business, real estate, or community development finance.[12] Reviewers receive an applicant's entire NMTC application, including applicant information that identifies the applicant CDE's type and the amount of total assets held by the CDE. If the applicant has a controlling entity, similar information is provided to the reviewers about the controlling entity.

Each application is reviewed by three external reviewers and, if the CDFI Fund identifies a scoring anomaly by one of the reviewers, a fourth reviewer also reviews and scores the application. Applications are scored based on a range of criteria, and applicants can receive scores of up to 25 points by each reviewer in each of the following four sections: (1) business strategy, (2) community impact, (3) management capacity, and (4) capitalization strategy. Applicants can also receive up to 10 "priority" points by demonstrating a record of successful investment in disadvantaged communities or businesses (up to 5 points) and by investing in businesses unrelated to the applicant (5 points). By agreeing to invest in unrelated entities, CDEs cannot own more than 50 percent of the QALICBs in which they invest. However, priority points are not included in calculating an applicant's score until the second phase of the application review process.

CDEs that meet or exceed an overall scoring threshold and a threshold in each of the four application sections advance to a second phase of the application process in which CDFI Fund officials determine—based on a final ranking score—which CDEs will receive allocations and how much they will receive.[13] The final ranking score is the sum of the aggregate business strategy score, the community impact score, and half of the priority points that a CDE received for demonstrating a track record of successful investment in low-income communities and investing in unrelated entities.

To determine how much allocation authority a CDE will receive, CDFI Fund staff review the amount of allocation authority that the CDE requested and, based on the information in the application materials, award allocation amounts in the order of CDEs' final ranking scores. When recommending allocation amounts, CDFI Fund staff members are instructed to consider the amount of equity investment the CDE can expect to raise in 2 years, the amount of NMTC investment in low-income communities that can be deployed within 3 years, the quality of the financial products being offered, and the projected impact on low-income communities or low-income persons. Not all of the CDEs that satisfy the minimum application score thresholds receive allocations. Allocation authority is generally awarded in order of final ranking scores until the allocation authority is exhausted.

Evaluating NMTC Effectiveness and the "but-for" Test

In evaluating the effectiveness of the NMTC program, a key question is whether the investment is likely not to have taken place in the absence of the NMTC. That is, would investors have invested in the specific project in the same location "but-for" the NMTC subsidy included in the project? Addressing this question is difficult because it requires estimating what decisions investors and developers would have made in the absence of the tax credit. Several methods have been developed that address some of the difficulties present in effectiveness evaluations. For example, statistical methods use control or comparison groups in an effort to determine what program participants and other potential investors would have done if the program did not exist. In a 2007 report, we used methods like these to analyze the effect of the NMTC on investor behavior.[14] Making definitive assessments about the extent to which benefits flow to targeted communities as a direct result of NMTC investments presents challenges. For example, the small size of the projects relative to the total economic activity within an area or areas eligible for the credit makes it difficult to detect the separate effect of the project.[15] (For the NMTC program, 39 percent of the census tracts qualify and 36 percent of the U.S. population lives in these census tracts.) Many of the eligible communities may already have significant business activities that could mask NMTC impacts. Limitations associated with available data and the application of statistical techniques also make it difficult to determine whether benefits generated in a low-income community outside the scope of a particular project are the direct result of the NMTC program. As a result, the analysis included in this report is limited to providing some examples of how CDEs participating in the NMTC program themselves apply a "but-for" test when selecting projects for NMTC investment. By applying these tests, CDEs attempt to identify and direct investment to projects in low-income communities that might not be feasible without NMTC assistance.

CDEs Made NMTC Investments, Which Generally Fill Gaps in Project Financing, in All 50 States, Primarily Investing in Real Estate

Through fiscal year 2008, CDEs reported making about $12 billion in NMTC investments (on which investors can claim tax credits totaling 39 percent) to about 2,111 projects located in all 50 states, the District of Columbia, and Puerto Rico.

California received just over $1.2 billion in NMTC investment, the most of any state, which was nearly 10 percent of total NMTC investment. New York and Louisiana received the second and third largest NMTC investment amounts at just under $1.2 billion and $863 million, respectively. Table 1 shows the 10 states that received the most NMTC investment measured in dollars from 2003 through 2008.

Table 1. Top 10 States by NMTC Dollars through Fiscal Year 2008 (Constant 2008 dollars)

Rank	State	Total dollar amount of investment	Percentage of total dollar amounts	Number of projects	Percentage of total projects
1	CA	$1,208,528,336	9.6%	257	12.2%
2	NY	1,184,947,158	9.5	100	4.7
3	LA	862,539,451	6.9	96	4.5
4	MA	697,153,422	5.6	121	5.7
5	OH	575,835,516	4.6	172	8.1
6	WA	484,742,478	3.9	57	2.7
7	MO	464,481,135	3.7	57	2.7
8	WI	445,072,159	3.6	117	5.5
9	MD	408,771,561	3.3	39	1.8
10	NJ	388,761,424	3.1	44	2.1
	Total	6,720,832,740	53.6	1,060	50.2

Source: GAO analysis of CDFI Fund data.

CDEs also funded more projects in California than any other state, with 257 projects. CDEs made the 2nd and 3rd largest number of NMTC investments in Ohio and Massachusetts, 172 and 121, respectively.

Louisiana, as the third state receiving the most NMTC investment measured by dollars, also received significantly higher NMTC investment since 2005, likely owing largely to Gulf Opportunity (GO) Zone NMTC allocations to assist in recovery and rebuilding from Hurricane Katrina in 2005. On a per capita basis (using 2008 state populations) the District of Columbia received the most NMTC investment, followed by Rhode Island, Louisiana, Maine, and Massachusetts. Appendix II contains a full list of the number of projects and amount of dollars received by each state, the District of Columbia, and Puerto Rico from 2003 through 2008, including the amount of NMTC investment in each state on a per capita basis.

NMTC allocations are distributed widely across states and projects tend to be predominantly located in metropolitan areas. Measured in dollars, about 90 percent ($10.6 billion) of total NMTC allocations deployed to QALICBs were used for projects in designated metropolitan areas. Measured by the number of projects, 1,730 (83 percent) of total projects were located in metropolitan areas. In recent NMTC allocation rounds, the CDFI Fund has taken steps to ensure that additional NMTC allocation dollars are targeted to nonmetropolitan communities.[16] For example, the CDFI Fund now tries to ensure that at least 20 percent of its NMTC allocation awards are targeted to nonmetropolitan areas. Figure 2 shows the relative proportions measured by amount of dollars and number of projects for NMTC projects.

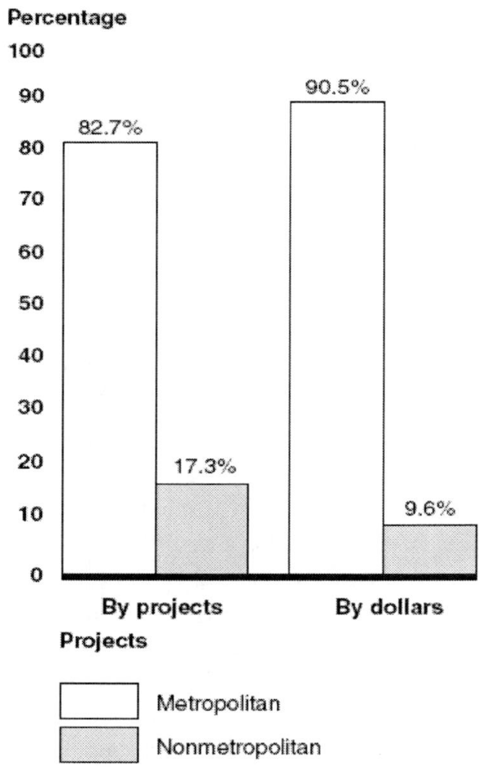

Source: GAO analysis of CDFI Fund data.

Figure 2. NMTC Loans and Investments in Metropolitan and Nonmetropolitan Areas.

Most of NMTC Investment Has Been in Real Estate Projects by for-Profit Allocatees

Although the range of activities financed by CDEs varies, NMTC investments have been used primarily for commercial real estate projects. As figure 3 shows, CDEs used about 65 percent of total NMTC loans and equity investments for real estate projects, although designating fewer NMTC loans and investments, about 22 percent, to finance business-related activities of QALICBs.

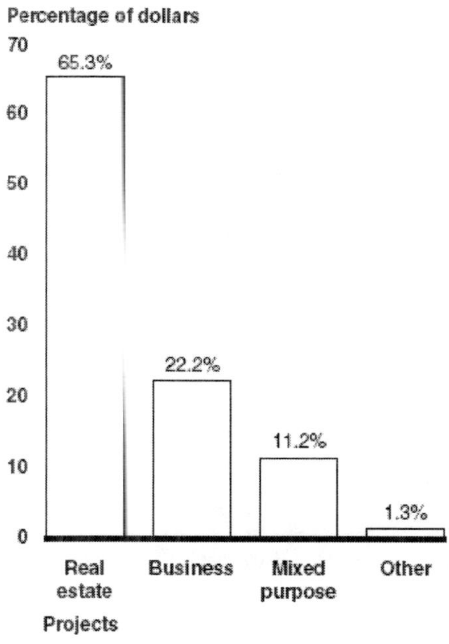

Source: GAO analysis of CDFI Fund data.

Note: Business includes the following categories of business-related projects: business, working capital, fixed assets, and microenterprises. Real estate includes the following categories of real estate projects: commercial construction and rehabilitation, and residential construction and rehabilitation of single and multifamily housing. The mixed purpose category includes projects with multiple CDEs contributing for different purposes—the real estate category includes mixed-use facilities with a single CDE contributing or with multiple CDEs all reporting real estate as the purpose.

Figure 3. NMTC Loans and Investment by Project Type.

According to our analysis of CDFI Fund data, commercial real estate construction and rehabilitation accounted for nearly all (about 98 percent) of the investment in real estate. Commercial real estate facilities may also include mixed-use facilities that have a portion of the building dedicated to for-sale housing or rental housing and a portion dedicated to commercial activities. Investments strictly in housing account for the remaining portion of NMTC investments in real estate—investments strictly in rental housing are prohibited under program rules.

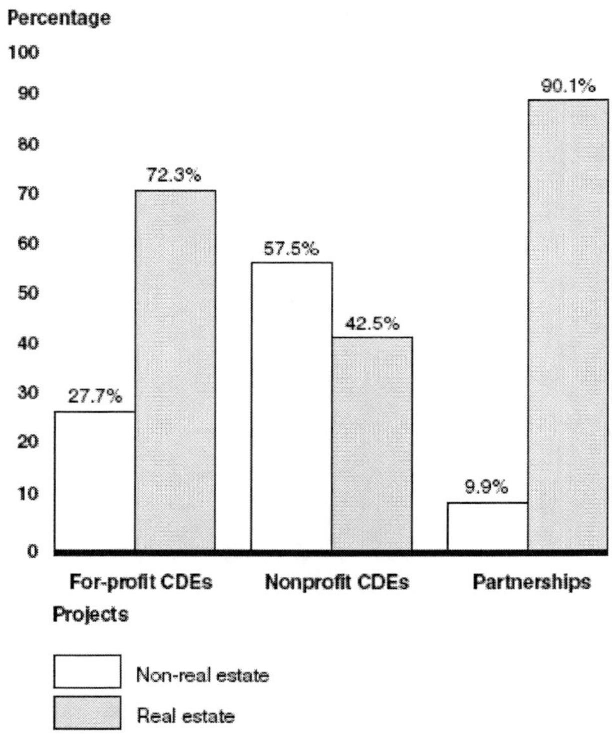

Source: GAO analysis of CDFI Fund data.

Figure 4. NMTC Loans and Investments by CDE Type and Project Purpose.

According to a recent paper developed for the Federal Reserve Bank of San Francisco, the CDEs have likely made real estate investment the predominant form of NMTC investment because investors see real estate as more profitable than other types of investment and less likely to fall out of compliance with NMTC restrictions. For example, real estate deals can often be more easily paired with other federal, state, and local tax incentives.[17] Representatives from CDEs we interviewed also noted that real estate projects are fixed in location, making it less likely that the project will fall out of compliance with NMTC program rules by moving the investment to a nonqualifying census tract within the 7-year NMTC compliance period. Furthermore, the investments are usually large and long term, making it unlikely that the investors will be repaid any principal on their investments within the 7-year compliance period, which would, by a requirement of the NMTC program, necessitate a reinvestment of the funds in another qualified low-income community business.

Although the range of projects adopted by for-profit and nonprofit CDEs varied across different purpose categories, CDEs established or controlled by for-profit entities (and partnerships between for-profit and nonprofit CDEs) made a majority of their QEIs in real estate projects. On the other hand, CDEs established or controlled by nonprofit entities made a majority of their QEIs in business projects.

Representatives from CDEs We Interviewed Said Most Projects Receive NMTC Funding to Supplement Funds from Other Sources

Through fiscal year 2008, our analysis indicates for projects with available data NMTC financing has been used, on average, to support about 36 percent of total project costs for projects that receive NMTC financing.

Due to limitations with project-level CDFI Fund data,[18] we were unable to identify what portion of each individual project NMTC investments supported. However, according to CDE officials we interviewed, although NMTC investments are unique to individual projects and the portion of the project being financed with NMTC funds varies depending on the amount of other funding available, NMTC investments generally support 20 percent to 30 percent of the total project costs for a particular project. For example, NMTC funds may be paired with other federal tax benefits, such as Historic Tax Credits,[19] or used in conjunction with state and local development subsidies, including programs such as tax increment financing.[20] Other projects may have access to funds from private foundations or individual donors. CDE representatives indicated that NMTC financing is frequently used to fill the gap between funds that have already been raised for a particular project and the total amount of funding needed to complete a project.

According to data reported by CDEs to the CDFI Fund, most investment made by the CDEs in QALICBs comes in the form of term loans. Term loans comprised $10.1 billion (85.1 percent) of total NMTC dollars distributed by CDEs through fiscal year 2008 to QALICBs. Participating CDEs also used debt with equity features, lines of credit, and other types of transactions, but these transaction types accounted for smaller portions of the overall NMTC investment from 2003 through 2008.

ACCORDING TO CDE REPRESENTATIVES, CDES OFFER NMTC FINANCING TERMS THAT BENEFIT LOW-INCOME COMMUNITY BUSINESSES; CURRENT MARKET CONDITIONS PRESENT CHALLENGES AND NMTC FINANCING COULD BE SIMPLIFIED

According to CDFI Fund data and representatives from CDEs we interviewed, CDEs generally provide beneficial financing terms by either using NMTCs to leverage additional investment dollars to place in QALICBs or by subsidizing the interest rate on a loan to a QALICB (i.e., charge lower than market rate interest on its loans). In the case of the leveraged NMTC model, at least some portion of the tax credit equity generated from the sale of tax credit authority to NMTC investors is generally left in the QALICB at the end of the 7-year period in which investors can claim the credit. Businesses are able to obtain loans from CDEs that essentially function as private equity and should help QALICBs refinance their debt into more conventional loan products after the 7-year tax credit period. In the case of the subsidized interest rate on loans to QALICBs, less equity, if any, may be left in the QALICB after the 7-year period, but QALICBs may save more on interest costs than under the leveraged model. These businesses require less cash flow to repay loans than would be needed in the absence of the credit.

Under the leveraged NMTC model, a tax credit equity investor generally forms a limited liability pass-through entity that obtains a loan from a bank. The tax credit equity investor combines its own funds with the loan from the bank (referred to as the leveraged lender) to invest in a CDE (makes a QEI) that, in turn, invests makes a qualified low-income community investment (QLICI). Because program rules require that CDEs obtain qualified equity investment from NMTC investors, the tax credit investor must obtain a loan from the leveraged lender—when the funds are combined in the limited liability entity, that entity then makes an equity investment in a CDE. In doing so, the financial benefits from the transaction are separated from the tax benefits; the leveraged lender receives interest payments on the loan to the limited liability pass-through entity and the tax credit investor receives a return on their investment by purchasing the right to claim tax credits on the total amount of the QEI.

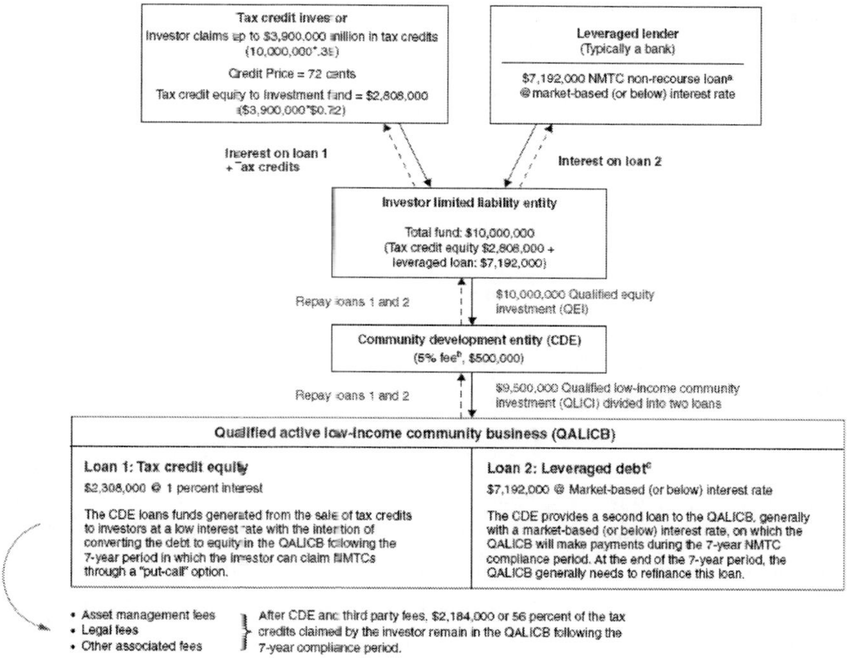

Source: GAO.

[a]The leveraged lender does not have recourse to the assets of the QALICB if it were to default on its loan repayments. Rather, the leveraged lender only has recourse to the assets of the limited liability entity formed to make a QEI.

[b]According to the CDFI Fund, most CDEs commit to invest more than 95 percent of their QEIs as QLICIs. For the 2009 pool of awardees, the average amount was 97.5 percent. Each awardee is required to meet its stated commitment as part of its allocation agreement.

[c]Due to the 7-year compliance period associated with the NMTC, most leveraged loans are interest-only for the 7-year period.

Figure 5. Example of a Leveraged NMTC Transaction.

The leveraged investment structure may offer a more attractive combination of risk and return to investors than the direct investment approach illustrated in figure 1. From the leveraged lender's perspective (as illustrated in fig. 5), this investment structure may be attractive because the loan-to-value ratio[21] is more favorable than it would have been if the debt was not being combined with the investors' equity. The more favorable ratio may compensate the leveraged lender for assuming a greater degree of risk, most notably if the business that receives the loan from the CDE defaults on its loan agreement. In that case, the leveraged lender's investment is secured by the equity in the original investment in the limited liability entity, i.e., generally the tax credit investor's contribution to the limited liability entity. From the tax credit investor's perspective, the base for calculating the credit is much larger than it would be without the participation of the leveraged lender and if the business defaults on its loan, the investor is still generally allowed to claim the full amount of the credit.

In this example, the tax credit investor obtains its return on investment by purchasing the tax credits for an amount less than the full value of the tax credits that it will be allowed to claim. For example, in a $10 million QEI in a CDE, the tax credit investor would be able to claim about $3.9 million in tax credits over 7 years.[22] If the tax credit investor invests $2.8 million in the limited liability entity, in effect, it pays 72 cents to the CDE for each dollar of tax credits that it will be allowed to claim.[23] The leveraged lender would provide a $7.2 million loan to the limited liability entity for the total QEI of $10 million. Once the CDE obtains the QEI from the limited liability entity formed between the tax credit investor and the leveraged lender, it then makes QLICIs in qualified low-income communities.

In general, the QLICIs take place in the form of loans to businesses because CDEs are generally required to adhere to related-party tests which require that the CDE have no more than a 50 percent ownership stake in a QALICB. Providing equity directly to a QALICB could result in the CDE owning more of a QALICB than is allowed. Representatives from CDEs we interviewed said that, as a result of the related-party test, CDEs generally offer two loans to a QALICB in a leveraged transaction (as opposed to one loan and one equity investment)—one loan that represents the funds loaned to the partnership by the leveraged lender (usually an interest-only loan for a 7-year period) and a second loan that represents some portion of the tax credit equity generated from the sale of the tax credit by the CDE to the tax credit investor (which is typically converted to equity at the end of the 7-year period).

The QALICB is responsible for repaying the interest (and sometimes limited principal) on both loans during the 7-year tax credit period. At the end of the 7-year period, however, the QALICB generally has the option of purchasing the tax credit equity from the CDE through a "put" option for a nominal fee.[24] The original tax credit investor does not generally get their original investment back because they obtain a sufficient return on their investment from the initial sale of the tax credit equity to the CDE. The QALICB should then generally be able to use the remaining equity generated from the sale of the tax credit to help it refinance its remaining debt into a more conventional, market rate loan with a standard loan-tovalue ratio.

Although, according to CDEs and other experts we interviewed, the ability to purchase the NMTC equity from the investor after 7 years is the primary benefit of the leveraged model to the low-income community business, the model may also generate other benefits. For example, by combining the tax credit equity and the leveraged debt in a limited liability entity, CDEs can raise more money to invest in low-income community businesses than would otherwise be available. CDE representatives also noted that using tax credits to leverage debt also allows CDEs to offer competitive or below-market interest rates on some NMTC loans issued to QALICBs. In addition, by introducing the NMTC leveraged structure, CDE representatives indicated it is often possible to obtain other incentives, whether from private investors or governments, including additional equity, for projects.

Structuring deals in such a manner requires QALICBs to obtain a legal opinion to ensure that the loans to the QALICB represent "true debt." According to representatives from CDEs we interviewed, this is particularly true for the loan representing the tax credit equity given that it has equity-like features[25] and the investor is expected to sell the equity to the QALICB at the end of the 7-year period in which the investor can claim tax credits. According to CDE and many QALICB representatives we interviewed, fees associated with obtaining such legal opinions and other expenses, including asset management fees[26] over the 7-year compliance period, reduce the amount of tax credit equity that reverts to the QALICB after 7-years. In addition, according to representatives from CDEs, QALICBs, and attorneys representing CDEs, QALICBs, and investors with whom we spoke, the fees generated by the complexity of NMTC transactions are not necessarily subject to the "substantially all" test because some are paid by the QALICB out of the proceeds of the QLICI or other sources of funds and not by the CDE out of the QEI, which is the point at which the "substantially all" test is assessed.

The amount of capital that is left in the QALICB is reduced by such fees, as well as by any reduction in the price that the tax credit investor pays for the right to claim the tax credits. The combined effect of high fees and lower price would be a lower net present value of the tax credit equity that remains in the QALICB after the 7-year period. The equity remaining in the QALICB after 7 years is the primary benefit of the NMTC to the QALICB under the leveraged structure because it should help QALICBs to obtain more conventional project financing after the NMTC compliance period is finished. Businesses that have considerable equity are more likely to have better loan-to-value and debt service coverage ratios[27] and are generally more likely to obtain loans with conventional interest rates than businesses without their own equity. For this reason, the larger the amount of equity remaining in the business, the greater the likelihood that the business will continue on its own without any further government subsidies. Because the equity remaining after 7 years is the primary benefit to the low-income community business, the amount remaining as a percentage of the cost of the program to the government is an indicator of how cost-effectively the financial structure is performing.

To understand the NMTC's cost-effectiveness, the CDFI Fund would need to collect data on the sale price of the tax credits, fees paid by QALICBs not subject to the "substantially all" test, and the amount of equity that CDEs estimate will be left in the QALICB at the end of the 7-year period in which tax credits can be claimed. However, because the CDFI Fund does not collect this data, it is not possible to identify with precision the net benefits flowing to low-income community businesses in relation to the cost of the program to the government in foregone tax revenue. According to representatives from CDEs we interviewed, such information would not likely impose significant additional burdens on CDEs in addition to current NMTC reporting requirements and would be readily available on a transaction-by-transaction basis.

Although complete data on the cost of NMTC transactions in relation to the equity left in low-income communities do not exist, our analysis of leveraged transactions, which is limited to those identified in our case studies indicates that the projected equity in low-income community businesses after the 7-year period in which tax credits can be claimed is about 50 percent to 65 percent of the amount of tax credits that the tax credit investor can claim over 7 years. All eight of the CDEs that were the focus of our case studies and participated in leveraged transactions generally agreed that it is reasonable to expect that the CDE will leave about 50 percent to 65 percent of the amount of tax credits investors can claim in QALICBs after the 7-year tax credit period and that the complexity of the leveraged structure is a factor causing less equity to end up in the low-income community businesses.

Because the NMTC investors are also required to pay taxes on a portion of their earnings from their NMTC investment and some QALICBs owe taxes on the equity remaining in the QALICB following the 7-year tax credit period, the total cost of the program to the government may be lower than the sum of the tax credits and the amount of equity left in the QALICB may actually be a larger share of total cost of the NMTC program to the government than the 50 percent to 65 percent figure cited above. However, the amount of tax credit equity left in the QALICB as a percentage of the total cost to the government also depends on fees paid and assumptions made about the time value of money.[28] In addition, to the extent that NMTC investors may not be allowed to claim all of the tax credits that they initially believe they will be eligible to claim, the cost of the tax credit program to the government would be lower. Other market conditions also play a role in determining the amount of residual equity that ends up in QALICBs—when NMTC prices are higher, more equity is generated from the sale of the credits to investors than when prices are lower, which increases the capital available for CDEs to reinvest in low-income community businesses.

In contrast to the leveraged structure, another common method for structuring NMTC transactions involves using NMTCs to subsidize interest rates to businesses in low-income communities. In this structure, a single investor (or multiple investors) may make an investment in a CDE and the CDE then, in turn, loans the money to a QALICB. As a result of the investors being able to claim NMTCs, the CDE is able to offer the loan at a below-market interest rate. The CDE generally passes the interest paid on the loan back to the NMTC investor. By combining the tax credits with a below-market interest rate, the investor is generally able to obtain a sufficient return on investment to justify the risk associated with investing in a low-income community business. Representatives from one CDE we interviewed said that the CDE can generally offer loans with interest rates between 3.5 and 4.0 percentage points below the standard market rates at a given time and in a given location. Depending on prevailing market interest rates for loans, NMTC loans under the subsidized rate model could be as much or more than 50 percent below market interest rates. For example, if an investor were to offer a loan to a QALICB at a 7 percent interest rate, subsidizing the loan with NMTCs would likely allow the investor to offer the loan at 3.5 percent or 3.0 percent, or about 50 percent to 57 percent below market, resulting in considerable interest savings to the QALICB. Although this is a considerable interest rate savings to the QALICB over 7 years, available data make it difficult to compute a measure of interest savings to the QALICB in relation the amount of tax credits claimed by the investor or whether the interest savings will allow the QALICB to save enough in interest over the course of the loan to be in a position to obtain more conventional financing after 7 years.

The subsidized interest rate model differs from the leveraged model in that no equity generated from the sale of the tax credits to investors is generally left in the low-income community business after the 7-year period. However, according to representatives from CDEs that we interviewed, the subsidized interest rate model is also less complex than the leveraged model and it may be possible to close NMTC transactions with fewer legal costs and other associated fees than in the leveraged model. As a result, the subsidized rate model may allow CDEs to finance smaller projects than can generally be completed using the leveraged model.

Current Economic Conditions May Also Decrease the NMTC's Cost-Effectiveness by Lowering the Price Investors Pay for Tax Credits and Reducing the Number of Investors

According to representatives from CDEs and CDFI Fund data, current economic conditions also may be reducing investors' appetite for tax credits, meaning that less tax credit equity is likely being generated from the sale of tax credits from CDEs to investors and CDEs, in general, are able to generate less QEI. For example, representatives from several CDEs indicated that before the housing market collapse and subsequent credit crisis in 2008, investors generally paid between $0.75 and $0.80 per dollar in tax credits. Under current economic conditions, these representatives said that investors may only be willing to pay $0.65 to $0.70 per dollar in tax credits. One CDE indicated that it has sold NMTCs to investors for as low as $0.51 per dollar and another CDE indicated that it had heard of NMTCs being sold for as low as $0.48. These lower prices to obtain NMTCs also imply that the amount of subsidy reaching the QALICBs has declined significantly.

In addition, as figure 6 shows, NMTC investment in 2009 is likely to be less than in 2007 and 2008, which may be partially due to current credit market conditions. As of the end of 2009, CDEs had raised about $2.4 billion in QEI during calendar year 2009.[29] According to representatives from CDEs we interviewed, when demand for the credit is lower, CDEs are more likely to sell tax credits to investors at reduced prices.

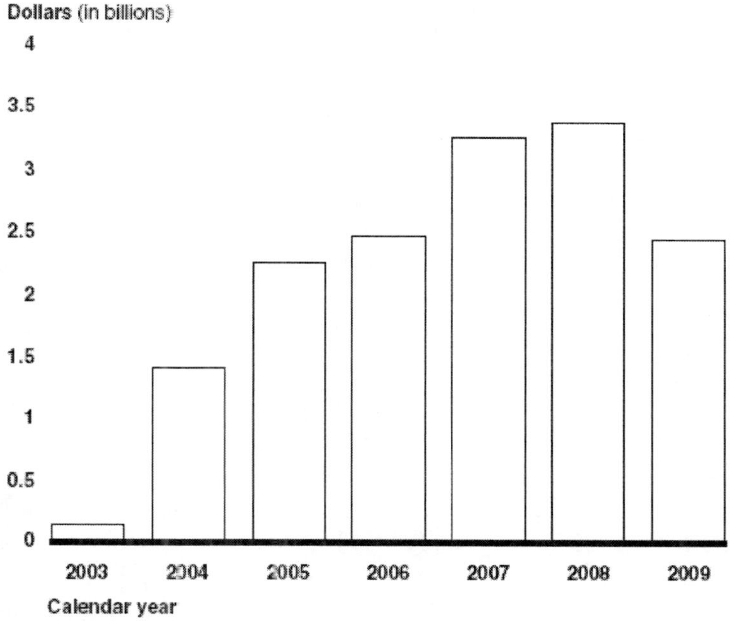

Source: GAO analysis of CDFI Fund data.

Figure 6. NMTC Investment by Calendar Year, 2003 through 2009.

To increase the number of investors, industry organizations and CDEs have offered several policy options. Some have suggested that allowing NMTC investments to offset alternative minimum tax (AMT)[30] liability would broaden the pool of potential investors. For example, while NMTCs cannot be used to offset AMT liability, other tax incentives for community development, including Low-Income Housing Tax Credits for rental housing and the Historic Rehabilitation Credit, can be used to offset AMT liability. If such an allowance increased the pool of investors and the price investors are willing to pay for the credit, it might have the beneficial effect of ensuring that a larger portion of the subsidy ended up in QALICBs. However, such an allowance would increase federal revenue losses to the extent that investors subject to the AMT who are not currently investing in NMTCs become NMTC investors and claim credits that would otherwise go unclaimed. Our analysis did not address whether such changes would likely increase the number of likely NMTC investors, contribute to increased NMTC investment, or assist in increasing the amount that investors are willing to pay for NMTCs.

Although It Is Unclear Whether Low-Income Community Projects Would Occur "but-for" the NMTC, According to CDE Representatives, CDEs Use a Variety of Methods to Determine if Low-Income Community Businesses Need NMTC Financing

Representatives from CDEs we interviewed indicated that the "but-for" test can be applied in a variety of different ways. For example, some CDEs require businesses to demonstrate that they have not otherwise been able to obtain financing before considering whether it would be appropriate to provide NMTC funds to a business. CDEs may also require potential beneficiaries of NMTC funds to complete a questionnaire that CDEs use to assess the likelihood that other forms of financing may be available. Representatives from other CDEs we interviewed indicated that they review their ongoing list of potential projects, often referred to as their project pipeline, to make assessments about which businesses or development projects require NMTC financing. Some CDEs may apply for an NMTC allocation with a specific project in mind for which they have tried to obtain financing in the past.

However, evidence we gathered was inconclusive in corroborating that procedures used by CDEs target funding only to projects that would not have otherwise been done. On the one hand, in most cases, representatives from CDEs and businesses we interviewed indicated that alternative sources of financing were not available to finance their respective projects. On the other hand, in two cases, businesses that had obtained NMTC financing said that alternative sources of financing would have been available for their project, but that the terms and conditions offered as a result of the NMTC financing made their respective projects less expensive and the use of NMTCs was more attractive than other sources of financing. In addition, although low-income community businesses may be benefiting from NMTC financing, it is not always clear how much better the terms and conditions being offered are than would otherwise be available. For example, representatives from CDEs we interviewed indicated that it is sometimes difficult to identify standard market-based interest rates to make comparisons across projects. CDE representatives indicated that prevailing, standard market interest rates vary by industry type, geographic location, and over time.

The CDFI Fund requires that CDEs commit to providing financial products to QALICBs that contain better rates and terms than the QALICBs would be able to obtain in the absence of NMTCs being part of the deal structure (CDEs make this commitment when they sign allocation agreements with the CDFI Fund after being notified that they received an NMTC allocation). The CDFI Fund prioritizes equity or equity-like investments and below-market interest rate loans as generally providing the greatest benefits to low-income community businesses. The CDFI Fund also collects information on other measurements indicative of flexible financial products, such as lower than standard debt-service coverage ratios, higher than standard loan-to-value ratios, and other measurements.[31]

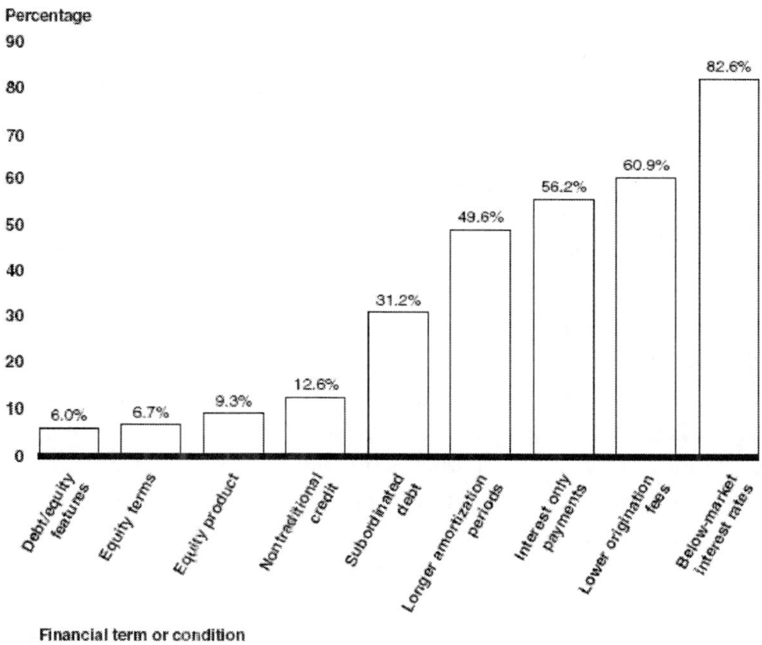

Source: GAO analysis of CDFI Fund data.

Figure 7. Percentage of Flexible Rates and Terms Reported by CDEs Used in NMTC Products, Fiscal Year 2003 to Fiscal Year 2008.

As figure 7 shows, CDEs report providing equity or equity equivalent terms and conditions (first three columns in the figure) for about 22 percent of financial products that include NMTC financing. Below-market interest rates on loans are the most common type of flexible financial product being offered. About 82 percent of financial products that CDEs report to the CDFI Fund indicate that QALICBs have received below-market interest rate loans. In the case of leveraged transactions, the loan made by the tax credit equity investor is generally far below market interest rates and the loan from the leveraged lender is at a more standard interest rate, although lower than what would have been attainable in the absence of the NMTCs. In addition, the large number of loans in comparison to other equity investments does not reflect the portion of those loans designed to essentially function as private equity under the leveraged model.

Options for Simplifying NMTC Transaction Structures

Although the NMTC's authorizing legislation and legislative history provide little explicit information on the program's intent, the NMTC program seems designed to increase the amount of investment, particularly equity investment, available to businesses in low-income communities where conventional access to credit has traditionally been limited. While our analysis does not allow us to draw conclusions about what would have happened in low-income communities absent the credit, to the extent the NMTC program subsidizes projects that would not otherwise have occurred, businesses benefiting from both leveraged and subsidized interest rate NMTC investments may be aiding in the development of low-income communities. To increase the effectiveness of how NMTC funds are dispensed to low-income businesses, changes to the application of the related entities test or replacing the tax credit with a grant are two options that could simplify NMTC transaction structures and increase the amount of equity investment available to low-income businesses.

Option One

According to representatives from CDEs we interviewed, economic development experts, and attorneys and accountants that execute NMTC transactions and based on actual transactions we reviewed through our case studies, the leveraged investment model is the structure that most directly develops equity in low-income community businesses. Though the leveraged NMTC investment model is structured to leave equity in low-income community businesses at the end of the 7-year loan period, the transaction's complex structure and its associated costs (in the form of the return on investment to tax credit investors and associated fees), raises questions about whether this is the most effective way to subsidize the creation of equity in low-income community businesses. According to representatives from CDEs we interviewed, identifying ways to streamline the leveraged model may result in CDEs placing more investment in QALICBs at the beginning of the 7-year period while incurring fewer fees and related costs that reduce the amount of tax credit equity that ultimately reverts to the QALICB under the current structure. According to representatives from CDEs and lawyers who developed rules for implementing the leveraged structure while working at IRS, one change that would reduce the complexity of leveraged transactions would be to apply the related parties test before the QLICI is made rather than afterwards, as is currently the case. This would allow CDEs to hold equity stakes in QALICBs in excess of the current 50 percent limit provided the CDE (or its investors) did not have more than 50 percent ownership of the QALICB before making the QLICI. The CDFI Fund is considering changes to the related entities test.[32] Although this would somewhat increase the equity that can be left in low-income businesses, it would not address the major factor—the sale of the tax credits—which reduces equity that ultimately is left in the businesses.

Option Two

According to our analysis, replacing the tax credit with a grant likely would increase the equity that could be placed in low-income businesses and make the federal subsidy more cost-effective. When the demand for NMTCs was highest, the credits sold for $0.75 to $0.80 per dollar. Therefore, the federal subsidy intended to assist low-income businesses was reduced by 20 percent to 25 percent before any funds were made available to CDEs. With low demand for the tax credits, as has recently been the case, the credits sold for as low as $0.50 cents, or lower, halving or more the amount of federal subsidy available to CDEs for investment in low-income businesses. In a grant program, these up-front reductions in the federal subsidy could be largely or entirely avoided.

A grant program could take various forms. A grant program could begin with the CDFI Fund making grants to CDEs, and then the CDEs making either equity investments in low-income businesses or providing them grants. Because the NMTC is structured much like a grant program—the CDFI Fund advertises for applications, peer review panels score applications, Fund staff determine amounts of NMTCs to allocate to winning applicants, and the CDFI Fund gathers information to monitor compliance and gauge program outcomes—the CDFI Fund likely could substantially use its current process for allocating the tax credits to instead allocate grant funds to CDEs. However, in switching the NMTC program to a grant program, some additional administrative costs may be incurred by the CDFI Fund and other interested parties, including CDEs and investors. For example, the Fund and CDEs would have responsibilities related to tracking costs associated with the grants to ensure only applicable costs are funded by the grant. Whether these costs would be greater or lesser than costs for the current tax credit program would depend somewhat on the design of any grant program. CDEs would continue to play a critical role in selecting and monitoring projects.

To ensure that the federal subsidy remains in the business, whether the CDE then made an equity investment (owns part of the business) or a grant (has no ownership interest) to the low-income business, those funds ultimately would be left in the business. In either case, to ensure that the business has at least as much funding up front as it receives in the NMTC structure, a private lender would need to loan funds to the business.[33] The CDEs could either broker this loan, somewhat as they do in the current structure, or the business itself could go into the market for a loan using the equity investment or grant received from the CDE as collateral. The program could be structured so that the lender may have recourse to the assets of the QALICB in the case of a bankruptcy, which is currently not generally the case under the leveraged model. In the latter case, the CDE might provide advice to the business. Involvement of the CDE in assisting the low-income business might be made a requirement of the equity investment or grant since that business may be inexperienced in obtaining significant credit. In our case studies, we heard that some lenders were more confident in making loans because they knew and had confidence in the CDEs, including that the CDEs would be monitoring the low-income businesses throughout the lending period. Requiring CDE involvement in obtaining financing for the low-income business and subsequently monitoring the business might therefore facilitate lending that would not otherwise occur or that would not occur on as favorable terms.

Regardless of how funds would be made available to businesses from CDEs, because more of the federal subsidy should make its way to the low-income businesses, which could be leveraged to obtain additional private financing, a grant-based program could either provide more funding to the same number of businesses at the same revenue cost, or similar funding to more businesses in total. Further, by eliminating the tax credit investor, a grant-based program likely would have less complex transaction structures with reduced fees relative to the current credit, thereby allowing an increased portion of available funds to flow to low-income community businesses. In any case, reducing the complexity and associated transaction costs for NMTC projects might have the added effect of making smaller projects more viable. According to CDE representatives, because fees associated with the various NMTC transaction structures tend to be fixed and do not generally vary based on the size of the transaction, using the leveraged model for smaller transactions has proven challenging.

Congress has turned to grant programs in other cases where tax credits had formerly been used. For example, to fill funding gaps in Low-Income Housing Tax Credit (LIHTC) projects, under the American Reinvestment and Recovery Act of 2009, Congress is offering the option of allowing state housing finance agencies (HFA) to exchange LIHTCs for federal grants to subsidize low-income rental housing. Under this option, LIHTC investors may or may not be a part of the investment structure. In cases where investors are no longer involved, HFAs are playing a more significant role in managing the assets developed from the grants awarded in lieu of tax credits. However, because the price LIHTC investors were willing to pay for tax credits dropped considerably during the severe economic downturn, if they were willing to invest at all, temporarily structuring the program as a grant program rather than a tax credit may be more cost-effective from the government's perspective than continuing to sell tax credits for fractions on the dollar.

Table 2. Options for Simplifying the NMTC Program

Option	Who makes the change	Examples of potential benefits	Examples of potential issues
1. Change the point at which the related entities test is applied from after the QLICI is made to before the QLICI is made.	Treasury	• Would make it easier for CDEs to make equity investments in QALICBs. • Would reduce costs associated with "true debt"analysis for leveraged loans and, as a result, would likely make more investment available to QALICBs. • By reducing fees, would make smaller projects more feasible than under the current structure.	• Need to ensure that safeguards are in place to prevent investors from investing in their own businesses. • Continues to rely on the sale of the tax credits to subsidize low-income community businesses.

Table 2. (Continued)

Option	Who makes the change	Examples of potential benefits	Examples of potential issues
2. Make grants to CDEs that, in turn, make equity investments in or provide grants to QALICBs.	Congress and Treasury	• Should increase the portion of the subsidy that goes to low-income communities by eliminating the sale of tax credits. •Would maintain the flexibility CDEs currently have in selecting projects to fund. • Would continue to rely on the administrative structure established by the CDFI Fund to administer the NMTC. • By reducing complexity of the structure, fees would be reduced and smaller projects would be more feasible than under the current model.	• Would need to change the related entities test if CDEs are allowed to make equity investment in QALICBs. •Would need to calibrate the allocation amounts available to ensure that the cost of the grant program to the federal government is similar to the cost of the tax credit program. • Would need to define the relationshipbetween the CDE and the low-income business in obtaining private financing for the business and monitoring it over time.

Source: GAO.

If the NMTC were to be restructured as a grant program, a number of design issues would need to be considered and the choices made could affect how well the program would perform and whether, in practice, it would be more effective at providing equity to low-income businesses and facilitating private investment than the tax credit. Consequently, evaluating the performance of any grant program compared to the performance of the current credit would be useful. Table 2 illustrates two options for simplifying the program and the potential benefits and issues associated with these options.

CDEs Use NMTCs for a Range of Purposes with Outcomes That Can Be Difficult to Measure and Vary Depending on the Project

Unlike some other federal programs, such as the LIHTC program which is used strictly to develop rental housing, CDEs with NMTC allocations have considerable flexibility in deciding how to deploy NMTC financing to low-income community businesses. In developing the program, Congress did not specify how CDEs can use the NMTC.[34] CDE representatives, in general, said that the flexibility associated with the NMTC is one reason why the program has been popular among community development professionals and low-income community businesses. As a result, the impact of the program varies depending on the project characteristics and it can be difficult to fully measure through data reported to the CDFI Fund. In addition to our limited number of case studies, forthcoming research by the Urban Institute may provide additional information on how NMTCs are used for a wide range of purposes.[35]

Our case studies of CDEs illustrated a variety of NMTC projects. In these studies, we reviewed NMTC projects with a chiefly educational purpose, such as an after-school program for at-risk youth in a low-income area of a major metropolitan area and a charter school for children with special needs. Other projects were intended to promote diverse goals such as housing and jobs, including a community center that assists low-income residents in obtaining housing and employment, and enhancing the health of community residents through medical facilities (e.g., hospitals and a doctor's office) in both a metropolitan location and a nonmetropolitan location. Mixed-use projects supported by NMTC investment also include commercial real estate, for-sale housing, and rental housing and appear to provide varying degrees of benefits to low-income community businesses and low-income community residents. CDEs have also identified and implemented techniques that allow for the NMTC's use in strictly for-sale housing projects.[36] Although it is clear from our case studies that low-income community businesses and residents have benefited from projects supported by NMTC investment, available data and statistical techniques do not allow us to identify the extent to which these benefits would have been realized in the absence of the credit. Table 3 provides a list and description of all of the NMTC financed projects we visited.

Table 3. Location and Descriptions of NMTC Case Study Projects

Census region	Project description
South	Multifamily housing facility that provides affordable rental housing and childcare opportunities to low-income persons.
	Single and multifamily housing units that will provide affordable housing opportunities to employed persons, living in high-cost areas, with limited capacity to purchase market-rate housing.
Northeast[a]	Community facility that houses year-round academic enrichment, sports, and community service programs for youth in the surrounding community.
	Community facility that provides comprehensive housing, community, and employment services to low-income residents in the surrounding community.
	Educational facility that provides comprehensive and multidisciplinary (i.e., psychological, social services, physical and occupational therapy) services to special-needs children in the surrounding community.
	Community-owned forest that provides local resource management andeco-tourism opportunities to the surrounding community.
	Mixed-use complex that houses a hotel, restaurant, and commercial office space.
	Medical center and hospital that will provide comprehensive health careservices to the surrounding nonmetropolitan community.
	Education facility that conducts research, community outreach, and youth programs on matters related to fishing and the environment.
Midwest	Single-family housing units that will provide affordable housing opportunities to employed persons, living in high-cost areas, with limited capacity to purchase market-rate housing.
	Medical center and mixed-use facility that provides healthcare and other services to the surrounding metropolitan community.
West	Mixed-use development that will provide market-rate "for sale"and affordable housing opportunities, commercial office space, and publicopen space for the surrounding metropolitan community.
	Mixed-use development that will provide market-rate and affordable housing opportunities and commercial space to the surrounding metropolitan community.

Source: GAO case study analysis.

[a]We visited more project sites in the Northeast than in other census regions because we visited a large financial institution in the Northeast that participates in the program in a number of ways (e.g., allocate, tax credit investor, and leveraged lender) and we visited a CDE that focuses on investing in nonmetropolitan areas that took us to multiple project sites.

The variety of projects supported by NMTC investment also makes it difficult to devise and implement a set of measures that fully captures their impact on the low-income communities. Job creation can be difficult to quantify and may have different relevance for different types of projects. For example, the after-school program we visited included a $9 million facility financed, in part, with NMTC funds. According to the director of the after-school program, with the use of NMTC funds and other funds, it has created about 12 full-time jobs. The director and representatives from the CDE that financed the project noted that although financing a $9 million facility to generate only 12 jobs may not, on the surface, appear to be generating significant benefits to low-income communities, the after-school program provides counseling and physical education activities to a number of at-risk children each week. They also noted that the facility fulfills a need in providing physical education opportunities to children that are generally not available in the public school system due to a lack of funding. Representatives from the CDE that financed the project indicated that it can be difficult to demonstrate the impact of the program because many projects may be providing benefits to low-income communities that extend beyond quantifiable data, such as the number of jobs that a facility is expected to generate or the square feet of real estate being constructed or rehabilitated.

Other projects we visited, which may have the potential to provide benefits to low-income communities, are currently still in the development phase or have been slowed by legal issues or market and regulatory risks. For example, one CDE we visited used its NMTC authority for predevelopment costs associated with a relatively large mixed-use facility in a depressed urban area. Although the NMTC funds have been depleted, the developer has not yet been able to obtain all of the additional financing necessary to begin the construction phase of the project. The CDFI Fund's application process can try to limit specific risks associated with the management capacity or capitalization strategy of a CDE but cannot address such systemic risks as an unanticipated tightening of capital markets.

The CDFI Fund does not collect data on project failure rates and our limited number of case studies does not show how frequently community development projects supported by NMTC financing are never completed or end up in bankruptcy. If the projects are never completed, taxpayers bear the burden because failure to complete a project does not cause the tax credits to be recaptured. In addition, because the NMTC program is designed to support projects in areas where access to capital has been traditionally scarce and capital investment is considered riskier, it seems likely that certain projects supported by the NMTC may ultimately fail. Data on the failure rate of NMTC projects would likely give the CDFI Fund a better understanding of the types of projects best suited for NMTC financing and additional resources for making future decisions about how to allocate NMTC funding.

CDEs Report Data on Employment, Real Estate Development, and Other Outcomes in Low-Income Communities to the CDFI Fund

The authorizing legislation for the NMTC program does not require the CDFI Fund to evaluate the success of the NMTC program; however, the agency does collect data from CDEs about the outcomes associated with projects that receive NMTC financing. CDEs that receive NMTC allocations submit annual reports to the CDFI Fund through CIIS. The annual CIIS reports contain information about how projects that received NMTC financing (in whole or in part) may have contributed to economicdevelopment-related project outcomes, such as the number of full-time equivalent (FTE) positions by job type,[37] affordable housing opportunities, and other new construction and rehabilitated real estate development in low-income communities. However, it is difficult to establish causal links between QEI, QLICI, and these reported project outcomes. Consequently, we are unable to determine the extent to which any economic development in the communities receiving the NMTC investment would have occurred if the NMTC program did not exist.

Although the CDFI Fund collects information from CDEs on the number of FTEs associated with funded projects, the CDFI Fund had not (at the time of publication of this report) released this information with respect to the 2008 data—primarily because it had not yet fully completed the process of cleaning the data, including implementing changes to its data cleansing protocols, particularly with respect to projects that were financed by multiple CDEs. According to representatives from CDEs we interviewed, techniques to determine the number of jobs varied widely. Some CDEs use proprietary economic modeling tools or contract with third-party consultants to determine the number of jobs on projects with NMTC financing, while other CDEs relied on internally developed research methods or on input from developers and low-income community businesses. These techniques vary in their reliability. As a result, although self-reported jobs data to the CDFI Fund represents a solid step in tracking the use and accountability of federal resources, the data may not reliably identify the number of jobs associated with NMTC financing.

The CDFI Fund also collects self-reported data on the projected real estate square footage for projects with NMTC financing as well as data on rental and for sale housing units, the capacity of educational, childcare and healthcare facilities developed using NMTC financing. Although information on the square footage of real estate provides an additional measure of the outcomes of projects associated with NMTC financing, the raw numbers, in and of themselves, may not provide information about the full context of a particular project.

For example, according to comments submitted to the CDFI Fund by one research institution, developing real estate in low-income communities in some areas is much more costly and difficult than in other low-income communities.

Although the CDFI Fund collects project-level data on the self-reported estimates of outcomes, the data collection method they use does not allow them to clearly identify the estimated outcomes for each individual project. Specifically, in cases where multiple CDEs contribute NMTC funds to the same project, the CDEs often all report outcome data on the project in CIIS. Our analysis indicates that this occurs for about 18 percent of the projects in the CIIS database.

In such cases, CDEs can report duplicate and inconsistent data for a single project which can result in the overcounting or undercounting of estimated project outcomes.

The CDFI Fund is aware of this data limitation and has developed an approach to consolidate and aggregate multiple entries for a single project. However, the CDFI Fund's methods may not be adequate in all cases. For example, if four CDEs contribute to the same project and report the same project-level information, simply summing the project level data in CIIS would result in overestimating the outcomes for the NMTC program as a whole.

According to CDFI Fund officials, in these cases it is appropriate to average the reported outcomes from all four CDEs to estimate the outcome of the project. However, if a similar number of CDEs were contributing NMTC funds to a single project for different purposes and were reporting the projected outcome of only their portion of the investment, then attempting to correct for duplicate entries for the same project might result in underestimating the outcomes of the NMTC program.

IRS and the CDFI Fund Have Established Processes That Will Allow Them to Better Assess NMTC Compliance

IRS is responsible for ensuring that CDEs and NMTC investors adhere to NMTC laws and regulations. As we noted in our 2007 report,[38] to get a sense of how many resources to dedicate to the new NMTC program, IRS conducted a compliance study of CDEs receiving allocations in the first round, focusing on CDEs' compliance with the "substantially all" requirement to invest at least 85 percent of their QEIs within 1 year of receiving the investment. IRS officials said that they chose to focus on CDEs' compliance with the "substantially all" requirement because they believed that this was the area where noncompliance with NMTC provisions was most likely to occur. In response to our recommendation in that report, IRS established criteria for selecting which CDEs to audit as part of the compliance study to ensure that IRS was reviewing the full range of NMTC transactions and that the results of its sample would be as representative as possible of all CDEs with NMTC allocations. For example, IRS officials indicated that they attempted to identify a range of CDEs to audit based on characteristics such as the physical location of the CDE, allocation amount, the CDE's status as a nonprofit or for-profit entity, percentage of allocation invested in urban and rural areas, the percentage invested in real estate and non-real estate projects, and other characteristics.

Based on the results of its compliance study and the outcome of future CDE audits, IRS intends to make decisions on the amount of resources to dedicate to CDE audits. In 2008, IRS used criteria similar to those used to identify CDEs for its compliance study to identify which CDEs to select for audit.

IRS officials have also taken steps to ensure that only taxpayers eligible to claim NMTCs actually claim them on their tax returns. For example, IRS selected a sample of NMTC investors using CDFI Fund data from the beginning of the NMTC program until the end of calendar year 2004 to assess whether investors were claiming the proper amount of tax credits on their returns and to determine whether it would be cost-effective to identify all eligible NMTC claimants, including those investing in pass-through entities.[39] IRS chose this time period because the information was readily available from the CDFI Fund and correlated with 2005 tax returns, the most recently available tax returns at the time of the study.

Using its sample, IRS officials compared the amount of NMTCs that they believed NMTC investors identified in CDFI Fund data should be able to claim on their tax returns to the amounts that taxpayers actually claimed on their tax returns. This comparison showed little evidence of ineligible taxpayers claiming the credit. IRS officials found that in cases where taxpayers claimed more tax credits than IRS would have expected the taxpayer to be eligible to claim, the additional tax credits claimed generally resulted from investors carrying over unused credits from previous years.[40]

IRS officials also noted that it can be difficult to track the amount of tax credits claimants are eligible to claim in the leveraged structure because it is not clear from the data what portion of the NMTC investment is allocated to which investor. However, IRS concluded that it is possible to work around limitations associated with CDFI Fund data on NMTC investors to ensure that NMTC claimants do not fraudulently claim tax credits. For example, IRS noted that it can use the CDFI Fund data as supplementary information when conducting audits and CDEs maintain records of eligible investors should IRS need to recapture tax credits. Further, IRS sometimes reviews NMTC claims as part of its regular field audits. This means that IRS auditors reviewing tax returns of corporations or individuals that also claim the NMTC would seek documentation that the taxpayer claimed the correct NMTC amount. IRS officials also intend to continue to review claimants' tax returns when the NTMC amount claimed is significant. IRS officials concluded that the potential benefits generated from developing a comprehensive system to track NMTC investor compliance for each NMTC transaction would likely be outweighed by the burden it would place on taxpayers and that the above steps should be adequate to ensure compliance.

Our guidance on internal controls notes that federal agency management should weigh the costs and benefits of processes to provide reasonable assurance that agency objectives, including ensuring effective and efficient operations and compliance with applicable laws, are met.[41] Our review indicates that IRS weighed the costs and benefits associated with its NMTC compliance monitoring efforts and has taken steps it believes will ensure that IRS will be able to meet the agency's goals of identifying noncompliant CDEs and NMTC claimants.

The CDFI Fund is responsible for monitoring CDEs to ensure that CDEs are compliant with their allocation agreements through the New Markets Compliance Monitoring System (NCMS) and, on a more limited basis, by making site visits to selected CDEs. The NCMS compiles data from other CDFI Fund databases that track investor behavior and project details to identify when a CDE may be falling out of compliance with its allocation agreement. CDFI Fund databases rely on data that CDEs self-report to the CDFI Fund. However, the CDFI Fund has several mechanisms in place that help ensure that compliance data collected are accurate and reliable, such as comparing census data to self-reported CDE data for some data fields and providing written instructions and a help desk to call when CDEs have questions about how to report information to the CDFI Fund.

According to CDFI Fund officials, the CDFI Fund has conducted more site visits to CDEs in recent years than in the program's earlier years in an effort to monitor compliance. CDFI Fund officials said that they conducted five NMTC specific site visits in Fiscal Years 2008 through 2009. In 2007, we reported that the CDFI Fund conducted two site visits in 2005 and an additional two site visits in 2006.[42] CDFI Fund officials indicated that they are more likely to make a site visit to a CDE when they have reason to believe that the CDE is not in compliance with the terms of its allocation agreement or is in danger of falling out of compliance. Although these site visits do not yield generalizable results to measure CDEs' compliance rates with their allocation agreements, they do supplement the information that the CDFI Fund receives through NCMS. In addition, CDEs and investors may also monitor potential compliance concerns. For example, in our 2007 report, we noted that investors we surveyed were generally concerned about the potential that CDEs could be noncompliant with program requirements and that they play an active role in ensuring that CDEs remain compliant with NMTC program requirements.[43]

Since falling out of compliance with the terms of the allocation agreement does not trigger a recapture of NMTCs from investors, in cases where a CDE is found to be out of compliance with its allocation agreement the actions taken by the CDFI Fund are generally limited to measures such as barring the CDE from applying for NMTC awards in future rounds. In other cases, the CDFI Fund may agree to modify the terms of a CDE's allocation agreement so that the CDE will come back in compliance with the allocation agreement. In general, the requirements to which CDEs agree to adhere in their allocation agreements are more stringent than the requirements that trigger a recapture of NMTCs. For example, CDEs may agree to invest closer to 95 percent of their allocation in low-income communities when the statute requires 85 percent to avoid triggering a recapture of NMTCs by the IRS. If a CDE were to agree to invest 95 percent of its allocation in a low-income community and fail to meet that requirement, it would be out of compliance with its allocation agreement, but would remain compliant with the NMTC program's statutory requirements.

Our analysis of the CDFI Fund's efforts to ensure CDEs remain compliant with their allocation agreements indicates that the CDFI Fund has weighed the costs and the benefits to provide reasonable assurance that the agency's objectives for monitoring CDEs compliance with their allocation agreements are met, including ensuring effective and efficient operations and compliance with applicable laws.

CONCLUSION

Congress designed the NMTC to promote investment and economic development in low-income communities. Our previous reports on the NMTC program indicated that the NMTC appears to increase investment in low-income communities by participating investors, and the analysis included in this report indicates that the NMTC program supports a range of low-income community businesses and residents projects. The benefits generated from economic development projects supporting the NMTC program vary depending on the nature of the project and can be difficult to quantify. Applying statistical techniques to assess the benefits of the NMTC program to low-income communities presents challenges, in part, because such a large area of the country, and portion of the population, is eligible to receive NMTC investment. As a result, our analysis does not allow us to determine the extent to which these projects and their resulting benefits to low-income communities would be realized absent the NMTC.

The low-income community businesses and residents appear to benefit from projects supported by the NMTC. However, the NMTC program faces challenges should it be extended beyond 2009. For example, the complexity of NMTC transaction structures appears to make it more difficult for CDEs to execute smaller transactions and results in less equity ending up in low-income community businesses than would likely end up there were the transaction structures simplified. In addition, current economic conditions have likely contributed to lower prices that investors are willing to pay to purchase the right to claim the NMTC, which also decreases the amount of equity available for low-income community businesses and the amount of debt that CDEs can leverage based on the available equity.

Additional information on NMTC pricing and fees associated with NMTC transactions that reduce the amount of the subsidy ultimately reaching low-income communities would lead to a better understanding of the benefits of the program in relation to its costs. Such information would also give

Congress and the Treasury useful information to make assessments about how to best structure the program, whether through simplifying the current structure by altering related parties rules or changing the program to function as a grant, to maximize the amount of NMTCs that reach low-income community businesses. Changing the related parties rule might have the effect of simplifying the program. However, it would not address concerns associated with relying on the sale price of the tax credits to generate funds to invest in low-income community businesses. Improving available information on each individual project would also likely allow for a more accurate assessment of the program's impacts.

MATTER FOR CONGRESSIONAL CONSIDERATION

Should the program be extended beyond 2009, to ensure that the maximum amount of capital ends up in low-income community businesses, Congress should consider offering grants to CDEs that would provide the funds to low-income community businesses. If it does so, Congress should require Treasury to gather appropriate data to assess whether and to what extent the grant program increases the amount of federal subsidy provided to low-income community businesses compared to the NMTC; whether the grant program otherwise affects the success of efforts to assist low-income communities; and how costs for administering the program incurred by the CDFI Fund, CDEs, and investors would change. One option would be for Congress to set aside a portion of funds to be used as grants and a portion to be used as tax credit allocation authority under the current structure of the program in a future allocation round to facilitate comparison of the two program structures.

RECOMMENDATIONS FOR EXECUTIVE ACTION

We recommend that the Secretary of the Treasury take the following three actions.

Should the program be extended beyond 2009 and absent a broader restructuring of the program, to ensure that the CDFI Fund has complete data on the amount of capital flowing to low-income community businesses from the sale of NMTCs to investors, we recommend that the Secretary of the

Treasury direct the CDFI Fund Director to collect data that show the sale price of NMTCs from CDEs to investors, fees paid by QALICBs to close NMTC transactions, and the amount of equity that the CDE projects it will leave in the QALICB at the end of the 7-year period during which investors can claim tax credits.

To more effectively assess the outcomes generated by the NMTC program in low-income communities, should the program be extended beyond 2009, we recommend that the Secretary of the Treasury direct the CDFI Fund Director to continue improving strategies for collecting NMTC project-level data that clearly identify the potential outcome of each project without the potential for double-counting the outcomes of some projects or undercounting the outcomes of others.

Additionally, to ensure that the CDFI Fund understands which projects have stalled or are not going to be completed and whether the criteria for funding selection could be improved, we recommend that the Secretary of the Treasury direct the CDFI Fund Director to collect data on the failure rate of NMTC projects.

AGENCY COMMENTS AND OUR EVALUATION

We provided a draft of this report to the Director of the Community Development Financial Institutions (CDFI) Fund and the Commissioner of Internal Revenue. We received written comments from the Director of the Community Development Institutions (CDFI) Fund. The Commissioner of Internal Revenue did not provide written comments. The CDFI Fund and the IRS also suggested several technical changes to the report, which we incorporated where appropriate.

The CDFI Fund agreed with a number of observations in the report and agreed with our recommendations that the CDFI Fund collect additional data on the program and refine their current data collection systems. The CDFI Fund also agreed with our observation that the current application of the related parties test may have unintended consequences of limiting equity investments and increasing administrative fees associated with the NMTC program.

However, the CDFI Fund expressed concerns with our Matter for Congressional Consideration that in a future allocation round, Congress should consider testing whether providing grants to CDEs that would, in turn, provide funds to low-income community businesses in lieu of allowing investors to claim tax credits for making investments in CDEs, would improve the program. The CDFI Fund said that it is not clear that such a change will make the federal subsidy more efficient, indicating that the NMTC is likely more cost-effective than a grant because investors pay some taxes when exiting NMTC transactions. According to our analysis, the leakage caused by investors paying less than a dollar to purchase the right to claim a dollar in tax credits and the significant fees generated by NMTC transaction structures means that it is likely that a lower portion of the subsidy is actually channeled to the low-income community business than may be under a grant program. Even if a grant program were marginally more expensive to the government than the current NMTC program, which we are not certain would be the case, if a larger portion of the subsidy reached low-income community businesses, the grant program could be more cost-effective.

The CDFI Fund also said that changing the NMTC program to a grant program would require significant programmatic changes and that it could not use its current process for allocating tax credits to instead allocate grants. In the report, we acknowledge that switching the NMTC program to a grant program will require the consideration of a number of design issues and that changing the program could impose additional administrative costs on the CDFI Fund. We do, however, conclude that the similarities between the NMTC's current programmatic structure and other grant programs (application advertisement, the review and scoring of applications by peer review panels, determinations by agency staff regarding the amounts of NMTC allocations to winning applicants, and processes for monitoring compliance and gauging outcomes) make it likely that the CDFI Fund could substantially use its current processes for allocating the tax credits to instead allocate grant funds to CDEs. Although we agree administrative changes would be required, we believe those changes could build upon current processes. In addition, the CDFI Fund manages several grant programs already, making it likely that the CDFI Fund could leverage this administrative capacity and expertise to administer the new markets program as a grant.

The CDFI Fund also said that changing the NMTC program to a grant program could cause program compliance to suffer because the grant program would lack rigorous investor oversight. Although we acknowledge that investors have contributed to program compliance, under a grant program both lenders and CDEs would likely have incentives to provide oversight, perhaps even more than under the NMTC program. The involvement of lenders in businesses may increase under a grant-based program because lenders could make loans directly to low-income businesses and have direct recourse to the underlying assets of the business whereas under the current program the leveraged lender does not have recourse to the assets of the low-income business if the business were to default on its repayment of the loan. Moreover, as we say in the report, under a grant program the involvement of CDEs in assisting low-income businesses might be made a requirement of the equity investment or grant since these businesses may be inexperienced in obtaining significant credit. The importance of CDE involvement in program compliance and oversight was particularly evident in our case studies, in which we heard that CDE involvement, including asset management activities, increased the confidence of some lenders in making loans because they knew the CDE and believed that the CDE would monitor the low-income businesses throughout the lending period. The grant program could also include penalties for CDE's failure to make low income community investments in accordance with program rules.

The CDFI Fund also expressed uncertainty that CDEs will be able to attract the requisite debt at the same rates and terms as are currently available if the NMTC investment incentive is replaced with a grant, noting that the debt and equity investor are, in many cases, the same entity. Although our analysis does not address whether the same rates and terms would be available, the leveraged model was created with the intention of separating the tax benefits of the tax credit investor from the economic returns from the leveraged lender—meaning that the structure's design was intended to ensure that the leveraged lender would be able to receive a return on investment sufficient to justify only their portion of the investment. Further, according to several economic development experts we interviewed, because under the current model the leveraged lender generally does not have access to the underlying assets of the low-income community business in which the CDE invests, many potential leveraged lenders have been unwilling to participate in the NMTC program— particularly in light of current economic conditions. If a grant program were structured so that the leveraged lender had access to the underlying low-income community business' assets in cases where the business fails, it is possible that more lenders may be willing to participate in the program.

Although we believe the concerns raised by the CDFI Fund can be addressed or may not be borne out in a grant program, we do believe that these and other issues merit study if Congress creates a grant program. Hence, our Matter for Congress includes the option that the CDFI Fund be required to assess the results of a grant program in comparison to the tax credit.

Finally, the CDFI Fund noted its efforts to work with Congress to increase investor participation by allowing investors to use the NMTC to offset Alternative Minimum Tax (AMT) liability. This would help place the NMTC on equal footing with other similar tax incentives, including the Low-Income Housing Tax Credit (LIHTC) and the Historic Rehabilitation Credit. The CDFI Fund stated that this change would stabilize the current market of NMTC investors and attract new investors. Although this could be the case, our work did not address whether such changes to the NMTC program would have these effects. We note, however, that although LIHTC program investors are allowed to use LIHTCs to offset AMT liability, the selling price for LIHTCs has fallen to a point where Congress temporarily converted a portion of the LIHTC program to a grant. Furthermore, if investors were allowed to use the NMTC to offset AMT liability, the price of the credit would need to rise above its previous levels to negate the likely benefits of changing it to a grant program.

Michael Brostek
Director,
Strategic Issues

APPENDIX I: OBJECTIVES, SCOPE, AND METHODOLOGY

Based on consultations with your offices, this final mandated report: (1) describes where and how Community Development Entities (CDE) are using New Markets Tax Credits (NMTC) to invest in low-income communities and targeted populations; (2) assesses how CDEs use NMTC financing to offer favorable financing terms to low-income community businesses and describes options for simplifying NMTC investment structures; (3) describe how, if at all, NMTC investments support low-income community development; and (4) updates our review of how effective the Internal Revenue Service (IRS) and the Community Development Financial Institutions (CDFI) Fund have been in monitoring CDEs' and investors' compliance with the NMTC program.

To describe where and how CDEs are using the NMTC to invest in low-income communities, we analyzed the CDFI Fund's Community Investment Impact System (CIIS) Transaction Level Report that contains self-reported data for reported NMTC projects through fiscal year 2008. Specifically, we used CIIS to develop summary statistics for the number and location of projects. We also used CIIS data to summarize the types of projects in which

CDEs invest, the percentage and amounts of NMTC investments for different CDE types, the portion of total project costs that are financed through NMTC investments, and the amounts and relative percentages of different types of financing for NMTC projects.

Given that the CDFI Fund requires CDEs to report information on project characteristics and financing once a year, CIIS data may not capture the most current information for all existing projects. However, the CIIS data that we used represents the most current available information on the status of the program. For some analysis, we were unable to use CIIS data for all available projects because CDEs may not have reported information for all required fields.

We interviewed CDFI Fund officials with knowledge of the CIIS about the steps they take to ensure its accuracy, and reviewed the computer programs the CDFI Fund uses to generate its NMTC databases. We determined that the data we used in this report were sufficiently reliable for our purposes.

To supplement our analysis of CIIS data for each objective, we conducted case studies of nine CDEs. Specifically, we interviewed representatives from these CDEs and systematically collected documentation contained in CDE project files to learn more about how CDEs decide which projects to fund using their NMTC allocations. In addition, we interviewed local economic development officials, lenders, and other subject-matter experts to examine how projects funded, in part or entirely, with NMTC allocations may contribute to economic development in low-income communities.

To capture the range of projects supported by NMTC investment, we used a purposeful sampling technique to identify the nine CDEs for case study analysis. To develop our sample, we used CIIS and NMTC application data to identify CDEs that received NMTC awards during the 2005 and 2006 allocation rounds. We limited our CDE selection to organizations receiving awards in these allocation rounds to examine projects with NMTC investments that were more indicative of the current NMTC program structure. To identify similarities and differences in projects by geographic area, we selected CDEs that serve low-income communities in each of the four U.S. Census Bureau regions (West, Midwest, Northeast, and South). The four low-income communities we identified were located in Los Angeles, California; Chicago, Illinois; New York, New York; and Washington, D.C. We selected two CDEs in each community. To capture variations in projects located in urban and rural communities, we selected one CDE with investments in rural projects located in Maine and New Hampshire. To examine the potential differences in investment strategies between nonprofit and for-profit CDEs, we selected nonprofit and for-profit organizations for our case studies. We also selected CDEs of varying asset sizes to examine variations in organizational capacity and the execution of NMTC investments. We identified options for simplifying the NMTC program through interviews with representatives from CDEs, qualified active low-income community businesses (QALICB), and investors.

Our case study results cannot be generalized to the full population of CDEs that have received NMTC allocations. Because the nature of project data, how it is collected, and how it is recorded varies by CDE, in some instances we relied on testimonial evidence obtained from CDE representatives, which we were not always able to substantiate with documentation. Also, given the volume and nature of community development activities in low-income communities and limitations with available data and available statistical techniques, we were unable to establish a causal link between a NMTC project and the changes in economic conditions in a community.

To describe and evaluate the extent to which NMTC investments appear to offer more favorable terms and conditions to borrowers in low-income communities, we reviewed and described common NMTC financing structures and analyzed CIIS data to analyze the terms and conditions for NMTC projects. Through our case studies, we identified how leveraged NMTC transaction structures and subsidized interest rate transaction structures provide benefits to low-income community businesses. We also used NMTC investor data from the CDFI Fund to review changes in the demand for NMTCs by investors over time. In addition, we used CIIS data to identify the frequency with which CDEs report using NMTC allocation authority to offer more favorable terms and conditions for loans and other financial products. We used information obtained from our case studies to identify the processes that the CDEs we reviewed use to assess the eligibility and viability of potential NMTC projects, and to obtain supplemental information from NMTC project files about the favorable terms and conditions these CDEs offer in conjunction with NMTC financing.

To describe how NMTC investments may contribute to economic development in low-income communities, we analyzed CIIS data on outcomes associated with projects that are in part or in whole supported by NMTC investment. Through our case studies, we interviewed representatives from CDEs and financial institutions, local economic development officials, and other subject-matter experts in each of the U.S. Census Bureau's four regions to obtain information about the contextual factors that are important to assessing economic conditions in low-income communities. We collected and analyzed documentation from CDE project files regarding how the CDEs we reviewed assess the outcomes of their projects on the communities in which they exist. We also collected and analyzed testimonial evidence obtained through our case studies to identify and summarize how and the extent to which current economic conditions have affected NMTC program activities.

To describe and evaluate the effectiveness of measures to ensure that CDEs and investors are in compliance with the NMTC program, we met with officials from IRS and the CDFI Fund. We also collected and analyzed documents on the status of CDFI Fund and IRS compliance monitoring efforts. We compared the information obtained to GAO's Standards for Internal Control in the Federal Government to assess the effectiveness of measures taken by IRS and the CDFI Fund to monitor compliance.

We conducted this performance audit from September 2008 to January 2010, in accordance with generally accepted government auditing standards. Those standards require that we plan and perform the audit to obtain sufficient, appropriate evidence to provide a reasonable basis for our findings and conclusions based on our audit objectives. We believe that the evidence obtained provides a reasonable basis for our findings and conclusions based on our audit objectives.

APPENDIX II: NMTC INVESTMENT DATA BY STATE, FISCAL YEARS 2003 THROUGH 2008

State	Total dollar amount of investment	Dollar amount per capita	Percentage of all loans and investment	Number of projects	Percentage of NMTC projects
Alaska	$37,978,424	55.3	0.30	23	1.09
Alabama	71,131,651	15.3	0.57	10	0.47
Arkansas	22,351,073	7.8	0.18	15	0.71
Arizona	235,904,081	36.3	1.88	45	2.13
California	1,208,528,336	32.9	9.65	257	12.17
Colorado	142,265,617	28.8	1.14	59	2.79
Connecticut	101,027,293	28.9	0.81	10	0.47
District of Columbia	189,536,869	320.4	1.51	22	1.04
Delaware	64,490,138	73.9	0.51	7	0.33
Florida	146,387,678	8.0	1.17	29	1.37
Georgia	132,099,181	13.6	1.05	16	0.76

Appendix II. (Continued)

State	Total dollar amount of investment	Dollar amount per capita	Percentage of all loans and investment	Number of projects	Percentage of NMTC projects
Hawaii	286,195	0.2	0.00	1	0.05
Iowa	103,800,268	34.6	0.83	16	0.76
Idaho	22,465,154	14.7	0.18	18	0.85
Illinois	205,879,374	16.0	1.64	68	3.22
Indiana	128,735,168	20.2	1.03	20	0.95
Kansas	15,201,077	5.4	0.12	2	0.09
Kentucky	380,231,286	89.1	3.03	83	3.93
Louisiana	862,539,451	195.6	6.88	96	4.55
Massachusetts	697,153,422	107.3	5.56	121	5.73
Maryland	408,771,661	72.6	3.26	39	1.85
Maine	216,657,193	164.6	1.73	19	0.90
Michigan	273,872,011	27.4	2.19	33	1.56
Minnesota	349,942,905	67.0	2.79	79	3.74
Missouri	464,481,135	78.6	3.71	57	2.70
Mississippi	204,035,342	69.4	1.63	35	1.66
Montana	995,308	1.0	0.01	2	0.09
North Carolina	368,608,411	40.0	2.94	38	1.80
North Dakota	11,428,689	17.8	0.09	2	0.09
Nebraska	32,191,630	18.1	0.26	2	0.09
New Hampshire	48,373,626	36.8	0.39	6	0.28
New Jersey	388,761,424	44.8	3.10	44	2.08
New Mexico	30,112,118	15.2	0.24	4	0.19
Nevada	652,388	0.3	0.01	1	0.05
New York	1,184,947,158	60.8	9.46	100	4.74
Ohio	575,835,516	50.1	4.60	172	8.15
Oklahoma	264,840,433	72.7	2.11	48	2.27
Oregon	361,838,881	95.5	2.89	58	2.75
Pennsylvania	326,283,735	26.2	2.60	51	2.42
Puerto Rico	1,634,384	0.4	0.01	2	0.09
Rhode Island	236,870,697	225.4	1.89	25	1.18
South Carolina	116,486,899	26.0	0.93	17	0.81
South Dakota	34,652,816	43.1	0.28	4	0.19
Tennessee	133,702,989	21.5	1.07	51	2.42
Texas	284,996,298	11.7	2.27	53	2.51
Utah	110,284,073	40.3	0.88	24	1.14
Virginia	314,165,784	40.4	2.51	37	1.75
Vermont	5,023,705	8.1	0.04	1	0.05
Washington	484,742,478	74.0	3.87	57	2.70

State	Total dollar amount of investment	Dollar amount per capita	Percentage of all loans and investment	Number of projects	Percentage of NMTC projects
Wisconsin	445,072,159	79.1	3.55	117	5.54
West Virginia	63,637,250	35.1	0.51	11	0.52
Wyoming	15,917,456	29.9	0.13	3	0.14
Total	12,529,292,310	40.7	100.00	2,111	100.00

Source: GAO analysis of CDFI Fund data.

Note: Dollar amounts are in constant 2008 dollars. Per capita calculations are based on the estimated 2008 population.

APPENDIX III: DESCRIPTION OF PRIMARY USES OF NMTC FINANCING, BY INVESTMENT TYPE

Purpose	Definition
Business	Financing to for-profit and nonprofit businesses with more than five employees or in an amount greater than $35,000 for the purpose of expansion, working capital, equipment purchase or rental, or commercial real estate development or improvement.
Microenterprise	Financing to a for-profit or nonprofit enterprise that has fiveor fewer employees (including the proprietor) and in an amount no more than $35,000 for the purpose of expansion, working capital, equipment purchase or rental, or commercial real estate development or improvement.
Real estate	Financing for rehabilitation of office, retail, manufacturing, or community facility space. Financing may include acquisition costs. Includes mixed-use real estate that combines both commercial and residential uses. Excludes acquisitions without rehabilitation.
Commercial construction, permanent, acquisition without rehabilitation	Financing for: (1) predevelopment financing; (2) construction or permanent financing; or (3) acquisition without rehabilitation of office, retail, manufacturing, or community facility space. Includes mixed-use real estate that combines both commercial and residential use.
Commercial rehabilitation	Financing for the rehabilitation of office, retail, manufacturing, or community facility space. Financial note may include acquisition costs. Includes mixed-use real estate that combines both commercial and residential uses. Excludes acquisitions without rehabilitation.
Housing construction, multifamily	Financing for predevelopment financing, or construction of multifamily housing.

Appendix III. (Continued)

Purpose	Definition
Housing rehabilitation, multifamily	Financing for the rehabilitation or acquisition of multifamily housing.
Housing construction, single family	Financing for predevelopment financing, or construction of single-family housing.
Housing rehabilitation, single family	Financing for the rehabilitation or acquisition of single-family housing.
Other	Financing other activities not specifically defined.

Source: CDFI Fund.

End Notes

[1] Pub. L. No. 106-554 (2000).

[2] GAO, *New Markets Tax Credit Program: Progress Made in Implementation, but Further Actions Needed to Monitor Compliance*, GAO-04-326 (Washington, D.C.: Jan. 30, 2004).

[3] GAO, *Tax Policy: New Markets Tax Credit Appears to Increase Investment by Investors in Low-Income Communities, but Opportunities Exist to Better Monitor Compliance*, GAO-07-296 (Washington, D.C.: Jan. 31, 2007).

[4] GAO, *New Markets Tax Credit: Minority Entities Are Less Successful in Obtaining Awards Than Non-Minority Entities*, GAO-09-536 (Washington, D.C.: Apr. 30, 2009).

[5] The original legislation that authorized the program allowed for $15 billion in tax credit authority for the NMTC program through 2007. However, the Gulf Opportunity Zone Act of 2005, Pub. L. No. 109-135 (Dec. 21, 2005) authorized an additional $1 billion of NMTC equity for qualified areas affected by Hurricane Katrina over a period of 3 years: $300 million in 2005, $300 million in 2006 and $400 million in 2007. The Tax Relief and Health Care Act of 2006, Pub. L. No. 109-432 (Dec. 20, 2006) and the Tax Extenders and Alternative Minimum Tax Act of 2008, Pub. L. No. 110-343 (Oct. 3, 2008) extended the amount of NMTC authority available by $3.5 billion for both 2008 and 2009. The American Recovery and Reinvestment Act of 2009, Pub. L. No. 111-5 (Feb. 17, 2009) added an additional $3 billion of NMTC allocation authority to be split equally between the 2008 (retroactively) and 2009 allocation rounds.

[6] A low-income community is defined as a census tract (1) in which the poverty rate is at least 20 percent or (2) outside a metropolitan area in which the median family income does not exceed 80 percent of median statewide family income or within a metropolitan area in which the median family income does not exceed 80 percent of the greater statewide or metropolitan area median family income. After October 22, 2004, the Secretary of the Treasury was authorized to issue regulations designating targeted populations that may be treated as low-income communities and procedures for determining which entities are qualified active low-income community businesses with respect to such populations. In addition, the definition of a low-income community included certain areas not within census tracts, tracts with low population, and census tracts with high-migration rural counties.

[7] Community Development Financial Institutions and Specialized Small Business Investment Companies automatically qualify as CDEs and only need to register as CDEs rather than apply for certification.

[8] The Tax Extenders Act of 2009 (H.R. 4213) proposes to extend the NMTC for one year. As of the time of this report's publication, the legislation has passed the House of Representatives.

[9] "Substantially all" means that CDEs must use (within 12 months) at least 85 percent of investor proceeds in years 1 through 6 and 75 percent in year 7 of the investment. CDEs can satisfy this requirement by two methods: (1) direct tracing of investments to specific qualified low-income community investments or (2) showing that at least 85 percent of their aggregate gross assets (75 percent in year 7) are invested in qualified low-income community investments.

[10] Beginning in the year in which the investment is made, investors are entitled to claim the credit for a 7-year period with 5 percent of the investment claimed in each of the first 3 years and 6 percent in each of the last 4 years. Investors are allowed to carry the credit back 1 year and carry the credits forward for a 20-year period.

[11] For a more detailed explanation of the NMTC investment process, see GAO-07-296.

[12] The CDFI Fund requires reviewers to disclose any conflicts of interest related to applicants with whom they have or had a relationship.

[13] Applicants that meet or exceed minimum scoring thresholds (48 out of 75 aggregate points— each of the three reviewers assign a score out of 25 for each application section— in each of the four application sections and an overall aggregate base score of 216 out of 300 points) are assigned Final Rank Scores, which determine the order by which the CDFI Fund reviews CDEs for awards. This means that CDEs receiving average scores of 16 out of 25 or higher in each application section and average scores of at least 72 out of 100 points overall advance to the second phase of the application process.

[14] GAO-07-296.

[15] GAO, *New Markets Tax Credit: Implementation Status and Issues Related to Mandated Reports*, GAO-03-223R (Washington, D.C.: Dec. 6, 2002).

[16] The CDFI Fund has defined nonmetropolitan counties as those counties that are not contained within a Metropolitan Statistical Area, as defined in Office of Management and Budget (OMB) Bulletin No. 99-04 with respect to 2000 census data. Section 223 of the American Jobs Creation Act of 2004 (P.L. 108-357) further specifies that low-income communities include census tracts in High Migration Rural Counties with a median family income at or below 85 percent of the applicable area median family income. Section 102(b) of the Tax Relief and Health Care Act of 2006 requires that the CDFI Fund ensure nonmetropolitan counties receive a proportional allocation of Qualified Equity Investments (QEI) under the NMTC Program.

[17] Lauren Lambie-Hanson, *Addressing the Prevalence of Real Estate Investment in the New Markets Tax Credit Program*, Federal Reserve Bank of San Francisco, Working Paper 2008-04, Fall 2008.

[18] These limitations, which include instances where multiple CDEs report different project costs for the same project and lead to the potential over-, or in some cases under-, counting of project costs, are addressed in more detail beginning on page 35 of this report.

[19] According to our 2007 report, the NMTC is frequently combined with at least one other government tax incentive that can provide additional tax benefits to the investor. Respondents to a GAO survey of NMTC investors noted that they most frequently combined the NMTC with state and local tax benefits, but also combined NMTCs with other federal tax benefits, including benefits for rehabilitating historic properties,

environmental tax incentives, and tax benefits for Empowerment Zones and Enterprise Communities.

[20] Local governments often establish tax increment financing (TIF) districts to use additional property tax assessments collected from economic development projects to retire the debt that a developer had to incur to undertake the project.

[21] Loan-to-value ratio is the relationship, expressed as a percentage, between the amount of a loan and the value of the asset that the loan is being used to finance. NMTC financing may assist businesses in obtaining loan-to-value ratios generally associated with more conventional financing in cases where low-income community businesses obtain equity or equity-like investment from NMTC investors (the equity reduces the amount of debt that the QALICB must borrow in relation to the value of the asset the loan is being used to finance).

[22] Because inflation reduces the value of the dollar over time and because of the time value of money, the tax credits are worth somewhat less than the $3.9 million at the time the investment is made than the $3.9 million total over the 7-year period.

[23] $0.72 per dollar of tax credit authority x $3.9 million in authority = $2.8 million in tax credit equity in the pass-through entity.

[24] A "put" option is a contract that gives the holder of the contract the right to sell all or a portion of its interest in a security to a specified entity at a predetermined price. Conversely, a "call" option gives the holder the right to purchase all or a portion of an interest in a security from a specified entity at a predetermined price. In the case of the NMTC leveraged structure, CDEs generally structure transactions so that the tax credit investor may "put" its tax credit equity to the QALICB or the QALICB may "call" the tax credit equity from the investor, in either case, for a predetermined price at the end of the 7-year period.

[25] The loan representing the tax credit equity has "equity-like" features because a portion of it (less associated fees) is generally to be converted to equity in the QALICB after 7 years through a "put-call" mechanism.

[26] According to representatives from CDEs we interviewed, the fee structure of an NMTC transaction varies on a transaction-by-transaction basis. For example, in some transactions, QALICBs might pay asset management fees to the CDE to ensure that the QALICB remains compliant with NMTC requirements. However, the amount of fees charged by CDEs and other participating parties varies by transaction, as does who bears the burden of paying them.

[27] Debt service coverage ratios provide a measure of how much revenue a business tends to generate in relation to its debt obligations. NMTC financing, in some cases, could assist in businesses demonstrating more standard debt-service coverage ratios because when businesses obtain below market interest rates on loans, they generally have lower debt service payments than in the absence of the NMTC.

[28] In periods of higher interest rates, the present value of a dollar to be received in the future is worth less than in periods of lower interest rates.

[29] Although the 2009 figure is updated through the end of the year, CDEs have up to 60 days to report investment data to the CDFI Fund after the investments are made, meaning additional 2009 investments could be reported in January and February of 2010. However, even if the CDEs raise more QEI in the 4th quarter of 2009 than any other 4th quarter of the year in which NMTCs have been available, or about $1.3 billion (which CDFI Fund officials do not expect), NMTC investment in 2009 would be about 16 percent to 19 percent lower than in 2007 and 2008, respectively.

[30] AMT is a separate federal tax system that applies to both individual and corporate taxpayers. It parallels the income tax system but with different rules for determining taxable income,

different tax rates for computing tax liability, and different rules for allowing the use of tax credits.

[31] Other than equity or equity equivalent financing and below market interest rates, the CDFI Fund defines the following measures as being flexible rates and terms for NMTC financial products: subordinated debt, lower than standard origination fees, longer than standard interest only periods, longer than standard amortization periods, more flexible borrower credit standards, nontraditional forms of collateral, loan loss reserve standards that are less than standard, higher than standard loan-to-value ratios, and lower than standard debt-service coverage ratios.

[32] While the NMTC statute defines what constitutes ownership under the related-entity test, the CDFI Fund has the authority to establish the timing with respect to when the test of relatedness shall be applied.

[33] The grant funds might also be used to induce additional equity investment by private investors in the low-income businesses as an alternative to loans or in combination with loans. NMTC investments in low-income businesses currently help induce equity investments in those businesses in some of the leveraged transactions.

[34] Regulatory requirements preclude business activities such as residential rental property, golf courses, massage parlors, liquor stores, gambling facilities, and farms from qualifying for NMTC financing.

[35] The Urban Institute received a contract from the CDFI Fund to evaluate the effectiveness of the NMTC program. The results of its study, which includes surveys and additional case studies, are due in 2011.

[36] Using NMTCs to finance the development of for-sale housing presents challenges because when developers complete the construction of the housing and sell the houses to home buyers, the developer may be in a position to repay the CDE, which would be considered redemption of the original investment. Per NMTC program rules, the CDE would have to redeploy the original investment within 12 months or risk having the credits recaptured by the IRS. One developer with whom we spoke indicated that the CDE with which his organization worked facilitated a deal structure that would legally address these concerns.

[37] For projects receiving business financing, one FTE is a 35 hour or more work week. In calculating FTEs, the CDFI Fund instructs CDEs to combine the hours worked by part-time employees.

[38] GAO-07-296.

[39] While CDFI Fund data identifies most NMTC investors that invest in pass-through entities, after the 3rd tier of pass-through entities for a given qualified equity investment is established, CDFI Fund data do not always identify the actual claimant. For example, in cases where a taxpayer eligible to claim NMTCs transfers the right to claim NMTCs to another taxpayer, CDFI Fund data do not capture the transfer.

[40] IRS officials assumed that claimants would be able to claim no more than 5 percent of the amount of qualified equity investment that attributed to the taxpayer in the CDFI Fund data. Investors can claim 5 percent of their investment in tax credits for the first 3 years of the 7-year NMTC compliance period and 6 percent in the last 4 years. Because IRS used tax returns filed in 2005 and the first NMTC awards did not take place until 2003, all of the investments would have still been within the first 3 years of the 7-year compliance period.

[41] GAO, *Standards for Internal Control in the Federal Government*, GAO/AIMD-00-21.3.1 (Washington, D.C.: Nov. 1999).

[42] GAO-07-296.

[43] GAO-07-296.

INDEX

A

B

C

D

E

F

G

H

I

J

L

M

N

O

P

Q

R

S

T

U

V

W

Y